When the King
Was Carpenter

When the King Was Carpenter

by

Maria von Trapp

NEW LEAF PRESS
HARRISON, ARKANSAS

Other books by Maria von Trapp:

A Family on Wheels
Maria
The Story of the Trapp Family Singers
The Trapp Family Book of Christmas Carols
Yesterday, Today and Forever

Second Printing, January 1977

Library of Congress Catalog Card Number: 75-46021
International Standard Book Number: 0-89221-018-4

CONTENTS

Foreword

FOREWORD

How did this book ever come to be written? So far, all my books have had to do with my family. Well, this one at least began with the family, with one incident, fifty years ago.

Little Martina, aged four, didn't like oatmeal. (As this happened back in Europe, we called it porridge.) She used to spread her helping very thinly all over the plate, hoping to create an "almost finished" impression.

In passing by I looked down at her and said, "Martina, the child Jesus would never have done this."

Quick as a wink, she snapped back, "Did He have to eat porridge for breakfast?" To which I had to answer, "I don't know."

Now the whole little person was sheer interest. "What *did* He have for breakfast, Mother?" And, embarrassed, again I had to answer, "Really, I don't know."

Now came the weighty words, "Why don't you find out?"

Her question stuck in me like a dart from then on. And that is the beginning of this book.

At first I tried the "direct question" method. As we had on our estate a chapel and a residing chaplain, there were many visiting priests coming.

From now on I would approach each one wistfully, "Excuse me, Father, but could you tell me what Jesus might have had for breakfast when He was a child?" I was so convinced that they must have learned this in their seminaries.

Their answer invariably was, "I have no idea." (And I had thought that the life of Christ was the main topic of all seminary curricula!)

As my first approach to the solution of my problem did not work out, I thought of something else. If I, for instance, would have wished to know what kind of breakfast Mozart, Shakespeare, or even Julius Caesar, ate, I would look into a well-written biography of these people. Therefore, I went into bookstores and libraries and came home with *Life of Christ* written by many eminent theologians, but neither Pater Meschler nor Mauriac nor Ricciotti seemed the least bit interested in my question.

The years passed and we had come to America. For a while there were other things more important to be taken care of. But then my query flared up again when I found books now in English about the time of Christ. I had already begun back in Austria to jot down interesting items I had found in books, and now I found so many more.

Finally, I had compiled quite a collection pertaining to the everyday life of a Jewish family at the time of Christ: what were the mother and father's duties; how a boy grew from babyhood into adolescence in five stages, each with a name; what they were wearing; and finally—Eureka!— what they were eating. And there was the answer to my sixty-four dollar question: They didn't have any breakfast! They ate two meals a day: one in the late morning and the other in the late afternoon. And with this I could have answered Martina and be done with.

But there was so much interesting material collected already that I went ahead and finished the book. And now I realize that there will be many people who will simply read the book and be touched by it, having learned to know Jesus as a fellow citizen, so to speak, or a neighbor from next door. But there will be the others who will wonder, *Where did she find all this information?* And those I have to disappoint by merely answering with titles and authors, as much as I still remember. (Some information I found when I went to the Holy Land and came in contact with scholars.)

At the end of the book there will be a reference list. My difficulty is that I cannot say now from which book came which information, but these are the only ones from which I gathered what is now so pleasant for you and me to know.

1

A HAPPY FAMILY

His earliest memories are the days of Nazareth just after the return from Egypt. He must have been about three years old.

The voice of his mother, "Mary of Nazareth" awakened her family every morning at daylight, calling out, "Blessed be He who loveth his people Israel."

Joseph Ben-David, her husband, whom the child called Father, would answer, "Blessed be He who loveth his people Israel."

And that was the way the day started in every Jewish household.

The next thing was to make the beds. Each person slept on a narrow mat which was rolled up and stood in a corner during the day. Their little house had only one room, which was bedroom, dining room, and living room all in one.

As they put on their outer garments, Jesus could hear his parents pray. He was too small then to understand the words, but he knew that for everything they did throughout the day there were special "Benedictions" to be recited. By and by he learned them all. There was one benediction for waking:

"My Lord, the Spirit which Thou hast given me is pure.

Thou has created it and formed it,

And Thou didst breathe it into me and preservest it within me,

And wilt one day take it from me

And restore it unto me hereafter.

So long as the Spirit is within me, I will give thanks unto Thee,

O Lord, my God, sovereign of all works, Lord of all spirits.

Blessed art Thou, O Lord, our God, King of the universe,

Who restoreth the Spirits unto their bodies."

Then he heard: "Blessed art Thou, O Lord, our God, King of the universe, who raiseth up those who are bowed down."

There was a benediction for getting dressed: "Blessed art Thou, O Lord, our God, King of the universe, Who clotheth the naked."

There was another benediction as they washed their face and hands: "Blessed art Thou,

O Lord, our God, King of the universe, who removeth sleep from mine eyes and slumber from mine eyelids."

And putting on their sandals, finally they said together: "Blessed art Thou, O Lord, our God, King of the universe, who hast supplied me with every want."

All these prayers Jesus was to learn by heart when he was a little older; but the first sentence his father taught him was the beginning of their solemn morning and evening prayer, the *Sh'ma:* "Hear, O Israel! The Lord, our God, is one! You shall love the Lord your God with all your heart and with all your soul and with all your might."

Every morning at the hour of prayer the father would draw him close, and together they turned their faces toward Jerusalem. Only the men were required to say the *Sh'ma* twice a day. Women and children were exempt, but this family prayed everything together. Always Jesus' mother joined in—and for Jesus these were the happiest moments of the day when he could talk to His Father in Heaven and turn towards His House. Very soon he had learned the entire morning prayer and could repeat it with his whole heart.

The second part followed:

". . . if you listen obediently to my commandments which I am commanding you today, to love the Lord your God and to serve Him with

11

all your heart and all your soul, then I will give the rain for your land in its season, and early and late rain, that you may gather in your grain and your new wine and your oil. And I will give grass in your fields for your cattle, and you shall eat and be satisfied. Beware, lest your hearts be deceived and you turn away and serve other gods and worship them for the anger of the Lord will be kindled against you, and He will shut up the heavens so that there will be no rain and the ground will not yield its fruit; and you will perish quickly from the good land which the Lord is giving you. You shall therefore impress these words of mine on your heart and on your soul; and you shall bind them as a sign on your hand, and they shall be as frontals on your forehead. And you shall teach them to your sons, talking of them when you sit in your house and when you walk along the road and when you lie down and when you rise up. And you shall write them on the doorposts of your house and on your gates, so that your days and the days of your sons may be multiplied on the land which the Lord swore to your fathers to give them, as long as the heavens remain above the earth. For if you are careful to keep all this commandment which I am commanding you, to do it, to love the Lord your God, to walk in all His ways and hold fast to Him; then the Lord will drive out all these nations from before you, and you will dispossess nations greater and mightier than you" (Deuteronomy 11:13-23).

In the third part of the morning prayer the family professed openly to be God's people by wearing a special sign on their clothes:

"The Lord also spoke to Moses, saying, Speak to the sons of Israel, and tell them that they shall make for themselves tassels at the corners of their garments throughout their generations, and that they shall put on the tassel of each corner of a cord of blue. And it shall be a tassel for you to look at and remember all the commandments of the Lord, so as to do them and not follow after your own heart and your own eyes, in order that you may remember to do all My commandments, and be holy to your God. I am the Lord your God who brought you out from the land of Egypt to be your God; I am the Lord your God" (Numbers 15:37-41).

As soon as Jesus could dress himself, blue knotted threads were attached to his garments, as they were to his father's. Mary took great care of these important signs.

After their morning prayer came the recitation of the "Eighteen Benedictions" which everyone, even women, children, or slaves, had to say three times a day. Jesus was too young to memorize that long prayer, but he listened—and loved to watch his mother, who never looked more beautiful than when she was talking with

God.

Next, both parents began the day's work. Before starting the duties of the day, every Israelite had to wash his hands and pray: "Blessed art Thou, O Lord, our God, King of the universe, who has sanctified us by Thy commandments and enjoined us to wash the hands."

While the carpenter-father walked over to the workshop, which was in a remote corner of the courtyard, Mary would put on her long veil, saying, "Blessed art Thou, O Lord, our God, King of the universe, who crowneth Israel with glory." Then, taking her son by the hand, she would go out into the yard where the water pitcher stood, stopping on the way through the door to lift him up to the *Mezuza*—a little wooden box with a slit, fastened on the right doorpost. In the box was a small scroll of parchment on which were written some of the texts of the *Sh'ma*.

This scroll was rolled up and on the outside was written the name of God—*Schaddai*—so that it was visible though the slit. Each time an Israelite passed through the door, going or coming, he touched the Holy Name with his fingertips. Then he kissed his fingers.

Mary would now take the empty water pitcher and carry it on her head to the well. When Jesus was a little older he, too, had a small pitcher and was allowed to help carry home the water.

14

The woman of the house always supplied it—and a great deal was needed, because many times throughout the day it was prescribed to wash the hands—before a meal, before starting a new piece of work, or when returning from the town. So Mary made several trips back and forth. She emptied the pitcher into a great stone amphora which stood in their courtyard and held about twenty gallons.

When that was done, she went to the small hearth on which the family meals were cooked, with some glowing coals and thorny brush, she made a fire in the baking oven. Fire had to be struck with flint and tinder, and to have it go out was a real disaster. So a low fire, carefully stoked and watched, was always burning, and it was used to light stoves, lanterns, and torches. People would even borrow fire from a neighboring house and bring back some of the glowing embers in an earthen vessel. Only in utter necessity would one strike a light. But every boy or girl had to learn how to do it, to be ready for any such emergency.

Then they went into the house. The mother took two wooden bowls, one larger than the other—giving her son the smaller one to hold. Next she went to the wall where Joseph had fastened a wooden container. Jesus would watch fascinated as she removed the stopper and let three measures of golden grain run into the bowl.

When she had replaced the stopper, they went outside again and sat down cross-legged, one on each side of their little handmill. This consisted of two large, heavy stones—the lower one fastened to the floor, while the upper one had a funnel in the middle and a handle with which Mary would grind flour. Jesus held his bowl at the side, waiting for the flour to appear. How he loved helping his mother with her daily tasks!

When the flour was ground, Mary mixed water and salt with leaven from the previous day's bread. She kneaded the dough in a wooden trough until it was smooth. Then she covered it with a piece of linen and let it rise. After about an hour, the dough was ready. She took the trough from the baking oven, rolled up her sleeves, took a handful of dough, and threw it back and forth over her left forearm. This made it grow thinner and thinner until it looked like a round pancake which she put on the hot tiles of the oven. After a minute or so she turned it over, and when it was crisp on both sides, the first loaf of bread was ready. She kept doing this with all of the dough until she had a stack of good-smelling, fresh barley bread.

When all of the bread for the day was baked, it was mid-morning. Mary would carry it into the house and call Joseph for the morning meal. By that time the father had also worked for two hours and with good appetites they all sat down. But first, they poured water over their hands, saying, "Blessed art Thou, O Lord, our God, King of the universe, who bringeth forth bread from the earth."

Mary took a low, many-sided table that her husband had made for her and put it in the middle of the room. On this she set the basket of freshly-baked bread, a cruse of water, cheese and fruit. Now all three gathered around the table, sitting on the floor. Each took one of the bread loaves, perhaps eighteen inches in diameter, and almost as thin as a cracker. Bread was never cut, always broken. On holidays there was wine as well as water, and olives or dried figs with the bread. For the son there was always goat's milk, which his mother bought from a street vendor and kept in a skin.

After every meal they said:

"Blessed art Thou, O Lord, our God, King of the universe,

Who feedeth the whole world with Thy goodness,

With grace, with loving kindness and tender mercy;

Thou givest food to all flesh,

For Thy loving kindness endureth forever.

Through Thy great goodness food has never failed us.

Oh, may it not fail us forever and ever,

For Thy great Name's sake, since Thou

nourisheth and sustaineth all beings,

And doest good unto all, and providest food for all Thy creatures whom Thou has created.

Blessed art Thou, O Lord, Who givest food unto all."

After the morning meal the father greeted his family with a friendly *Shalom*—"peace be with you"—and went back to his work, while Jesus, like all little boys under six years of age, stayed with his mother.

There was another responsibility for the women in the family: they must provide sufficient fuel without spending any money for it. During the dry season, therefore, Jesus accompanied Mary every day out over the barren hillsides; and together they gathered thistles, thorns, and dried grass—good only for the oven. Later in the summer Mary would take along a basket for the dry manure (karavan, camel dung) of the pastures, best for kindling the fire. If they were fortunate enough to be among the first after the passing of a caravan the "camel pies" would be plentiful. (A favorite source of kindling wood).

In the spring she showed Jesus how to gather wild herbs for the cooking.

In the summer they picked figs and grapes, drying them on the flat roof of the house.

In the fall, just before the rainy season, there was the olive harvest, and they collected the ripe olives by shaking the trees and also using sticks.

The finest and best oil Mary made in a bronze mortar, held between her knees, as she sat on the floor pounding the olives with a pestle. This oil, kept in a special pitcher, was only used for the Sabbath lamp. In addition, there was oil for the cooking, and oil set aside to be used as ointment for wounds. Whenever Joseph hurt himself at his work Mary would pour first wine, then oil into the wound.

In Nazareth there are only two seasons: the dry season and the rainy season. In the dry season the family's living room was really the courtyard. There Mary had a big handloom set up under the trees. She thoroughly enjoyed taking her place before the loom. First she strung it with long warp strings of hemp or cotton, wool or silk. Then she used a shuttle to insert the horizontal threads, or woof strings, between the warp threads. With a large comb she pushed the woof firmly down.

At the beginning of each rainy season the father would take the two big wooden uprights which fastened the loom and move them indoors for the wet winter months.

Jesus loved those hours spent sitting next to his mother, as he watched her weaving, or spinning, sewing, or mending their garments. She would tell him beautiful stories of Adam and Eve in the Garden of Paradise; of Noah and the flood; of Father Abraham who almost sacrificed his only son, Isaac; of Joseph in Egypt; of Moses and the great miracles of God performed to protect his people from the Pharaoh; of the prophet Isaiah and Queen Esther; of Judith, the valiant woman; and of their own ancestors, Ruth and King David.

Sometimes, too, his mother would sing. She had a beautiful voice and loved the ancient psalms, sung by King David and King Solomon. Often she sang, "The Lord is my shepherd, I shall not want," but her favorite song began with the words: "My soul doth magnify the Lord," and always as she sang it her face had a solemn expression. Another psalm which Mary learned from her kinsman, Zacharias, began: "Blessed be the Lord God of Israel because he has visited and wrought the redemption of his people."

Sometimes she chose as a last song one she had heard an old man sing in the temple at Jerusalem:"Lord, now lettest Thou thy servant depart in peace, according to Thy word."

Mary also told Jesus the story of the three young men in the fiery furnace and taught him the hymn they had sung: "Blessed art Thou, O Lord, the God of our fathers, and worthy to be praised and glorified forever." This song was a long one with many verses. After each verse Jesus would respond: "And worthy to be praised and glorified forever."

In the evening after the meal, Jesus would

repeat to his father the beautiful stories he had learned, and liked to surprise him every day with a new story or a new song. Joseph never said much, but the touch of his hand on the boy's head showed his pleasure.

Late in the afternoon Mary would prepare the main meal which had to be eaten before sunset. Once again, of course, hands were washed before the family sat down, and the father said grace to which mother and son answered "Amen." The meal usually consisted of a stew of rice, beans or lentils, or sometimes cracked wheat with a thick soup or a sauce. Meat was only for feast days, but occasionally there was fish or eggs with the stew. The boy Jesus had his special bowl of milk, and honey for his bread. There were no knives or forks, only broken pieces of bread used as spoons and dipped into the same bowl. Sometimes the wafer-thin crisp bread was used as a plate, held in the left hand, while with the right they dished from the big bowl to the bread. Eventually the plate was eaten as well.

During the summer months, meals were taken in the courtyard. In this central place they ate and lived, and even slept through the dry season. Sometimes, when the day was especially hot, the three took their mats to the flat roof, hoping to catch a cool breeze up there. On other housetops they could hear neighbors doing the same thing. Before they went to sleep, however,

Joseph once again called them together, and with Jesus next to him, began the evening prayer, the *Sh'ma*. At the end, the father would say: "I bless you in the name of Jahweh," and Mary and Jesus would answer: "The blessing of Jahweh be with you."

Then, after a last *Shalom*, they took off their upper garments, stepped out of their sandals, and lay down, hearts filled with gratitude towards their Father in Heaven, who once again had bestowed so many blessings on them during the day.

Theirs was a happy family.

"TAPH"

What did the word "family" mean to the carpenter's son? Not only his father and mother, but his grandparents, all his uncles and aunts, even all cousins, though in their Aramaic tongue there was no word for "cousin." Blood relationship was so strong a bond that people spoke only of "sisters" and "brothers." The welfare of each and the decisions which had to be made by any individual were always regarded as a concern of the whole group.

Joseph's family, returning from Egypt to Mary's native town of Nazareth, had found there a large "family" group. Mary had a step-sister whose name was also Mary, whose first husband, Alpheus, had died leaving her with several daughters and two sons, James and Joseph. When this Mary married Cleophas, a brother of Joseph the carpenter, they too had several daughters, and again two sons, Simon and Jude. For the new arrivals, these, and Mary's cousin Elizabeth, were their closest relatives in the whole big group. Here in Nazareth, Joseph Ben-David settled with his wife and child.

Growing children were watched with loving care through eight different stages of development:

YELED, or new-born babe

YONEQ, nursed by its mother

OLEL, when the child begins to ask for other food

GAMUL, at the age of three when definitely weaned

TAPH, a child clinging to its mother

ELEM, at six, when his father starts teaching the boy and sends him to school in the synagogue

NAAR, at ten, "one who shakes himself free"

BACHUR, at twelve, when the boy is a "ripened one," mature before the Law.

While the boy Jesus was still a little *Taph* clinging to his mother, the peaceful years passed only too quickly. Small children, girls and boys, all played together in one courtyard or another. They did as all children do the world over: they imitated their elders. The girls played at cooking, and the boys went to the father's workshop. Jesus went to the carpenter's workshop to amuse himself with shavings or left-over pieces lying around on the floor. (There are certain old-fashioned holy cards where we see the boy Jesus playfully putting little pieces of wood into crosses. This was as impossible as if our present-day little ones would play hanging a man on the gallows. The cross was a curse, never a plaything.) The children also loved to play Sabbath, with the girls imitating their mothers in the preparations for the holy day, and, finally, lighting the Sabbath lamp; while the boys veiling their heads with any handy piece of cloth, would band together in a little group of "men," face towards Jerusalem, and recite as many prayers as possible.

They also played at marriage and funerals. For a "wedding," some of the boys would blow on their little pipes, and the others would dance. At "funerals" where they buried little animals and locusts, all had to mourn. When they felt hot from so much running about, they would gather in the cool shade of a tree to play word and riddle games.

For the child Jesus, clinging to his mother, the happiest moments were always those spent in her presence. Peacefully, he followed her around the house, to the well, and up and down the surrounding hills, as she went for firewood. In those years he developed a deep love for his mother. Like other children his age, he watched her closely and tried to imitate her. She was always cheerful, with a ready smile and if he hurt himself he would run to her, let her take him in her arms, and let her quiet his grief with the deep peace of her presence.

Once a week there would be wash day. For her family, Mary provided a double set of clothing for both winter and summer. Usually on Thursday she soaked the clothes, rubbed them, and hung them up to dry. The linen was always bleached in the sun, and for Joseph's working clothes there was a special mixture of soda and potash in the water. Of all their apparel, only the sandals were bought. Everything else Mary spun and wove herself.

Very soon Jesus noticed that she was not given to talk. While other women lingered at the well with lively chitchat about the news of the day, Mary would be an interested listener but never joined in such gossiping. With a friendly smile she would greet the older ones or return the greeting of the younger, then she would merely fill her pitcher and depart.

The boy Jesus was growing quickly. He needed a new pair of sandals as fast as he outgrew the others, which were then always given to a poor child. He loved to go shopping in the bazaars with his mother on market day. All the stores had their goods displayed outside on the street and arranged on tables. There he could see pottery, or expensive imported articles such as metal lamps from Corinth, and cloth from India's Chinese silks, precious woods, carpets and jewels. Butchers and bakers displayed their goods; fried fish, Syrian wine, glassware from Egypt and cheap pottery—all were on display.

Professional scribes had their booths to write letters for the people. Interpreters were always ready for the many foreigners who traveled through town with their caravans. Doves, pigeons, chicken, geese and ducks would make a great noise in their cages. Next to them, on a stand of vegetables, there would be onions, radishes, lettuce, horseradish, lentils, beans, carrots and chickpeas for sale, besides an abundance of fruit: pears, apples, dates, plums, nuts, cherries, lemons, pomegranates, figs, olives and grapes.

Many coins were used, especially the Roman denarius, which was equal to the Greek *drachma* (about seventeen cents). This was the usual day's pay for the laborer. The Syrian *stater* was taken as equivalent to the Jewish *shekel* (about sixty-four cents). Market prices varied: two pigeons would be about twenty cents; a lamb about fifty cents; a sheep about five dollars; a donkey around twenty dollars and a cow thirty dollars. A slave cost up to thirty-four dollars, and for five dollars one could buy a suit for him. A role of Sacred Scriptures, copied by a scribe, was as high as eighty-five dollars.

In their goings and comings together, Jesus came to know from his mother how very important were the greetings of his people. If two men met, both riding on a beast of burden, they dismounted. One might simply turn to the other or take a few steps towards him. A more solemn manner of greeting was to prostrate oneself, touching the floor with the forehead several times. Royalty was greeted so, or with a deep genuflection. Then again, for a prophet or man of God, one would kneel before him and embrace his knees. Only the greatest hurry or most serious duty would excuse one from bestowing a greeting. Failure to return the salutation was almost a curse. Within the families, children kissed their parents, intimate friends, and close relatives in coming or going. "The Lord be with you," one might say, at which the other would answer, "May the Lord bless you." A longer formula said, "The blessing of the Lord come over you," with the answer, "I bless you in the name of the Lord." Of all the greetings, the shortest and simplest was the single word *Shalom*—"Peace be to you."

And "peace" remained with the house and family of Jesus.

3

THE DAY OF THE LORD

When he was still very young, Jesus noticed that there was one day in the week on which his mother would double the portion of grain to be ground in the morning, and bake twice as much bread as on other days. That was Friday. It was done in preparation for the Sabbath when she would rest like all the other people in the Holy Land.

The Sabbath was their holy day of rest and worship. In all the homes, therefore, there was eager activity each Friday, with the mothers preparing Sabbath meals ahead of time. By afternoon Mary would have finished with the cooking, storing meals for the next day in a wooden chest near the stove in order to keep them warm. Then she would go over to a larger chest, which was very beautifully carved, a masterpiece made by Joseph for his bride, there she kept the Sabbath clothes. Now she would lay them out so that all might be dressed and ready when the Sabbath was announced.

Next, Mary cleaned the house. She had a broom made of special bushy dried twigs, and would sweep the whole house. When all was swept and everything else was ready, the Sabbath lamp filled with new oil, the clothes hung up, ready to be worn, Mary took what looked like a large rolling pin, knelt down on the floor opposite the house door, and started rolling the floor smoothly, erasing all footprints. An earthen floor could not be washed with water, but the rolling gave the room a fresh, almost new look. In all homes all over the land this went on, giving Friday always a special air of preparation and expectancy.

Every household had a number of wicker partitions, something like screens, which could be put up, to create small cells. Mary would put one up now and go in with her Sabbath clothes. When she came out, she always looked beautiful in her bright-blue upper garment with the linen showing underneath, and a fresh white veil over her head. Then she would dress her son. Invariably, after the benediction for the changing of garments, she said: "Listen for the sound of the trumpet!" Jesus would already be listening. From the top of the synagogue in Nazareth, where a man was watching the sky, three signals were given with the trumpet. With the first, at sunset, those working in the fields would stop and return to their homes. As the first star appeared in the sky, a second signal was given, which meant that all artisans, Joseph among them, and all shopkeepers should stop work. Mary and Jesus knew that soon after the second signal the head of the house would appear. Time was allowed for the men to bathe and change their garments before the final and last signal announced the beginning of the Sabbath.

At the third trumpet all three members of the family were ready at the door. Now Mary led the little procession, going over to the corner where the Sabbath lamp was fastened to the wall. The lighting of the lamp was always a solemn moment, and the way she did it filled Jesus' heart with reverence for the Day of the Lord. Then they settled down to their Sabbath meal, as Mary brought dishes out of the chest behind the stove. It was a feast-day meal. While during the week only one dish was served, on the Sabbath Mary had many different things on the table. Some of the vegetables, such as small cucumbers and carrots, were eaten raw. While she usually boiled vegetables in water, for the Sabbath they were stewed in oil. A dish of lentil stew was always wonderful, but on the Sabbath there was even boiled meat, usually mutton, in the stew. Sometimes it was chicken, or a kid, or a young lamb. There was fresh fruit on the table too: grapes, mulberries, dates, pomegranates, and different sorts of nuts. In winter it would be dried fruit. Dates and pomegranates Mary would buy at the bazaar. Other fruit grew in the courtyard. As there was no sugar, they used honey for sweetening. Mary had made little cakes and filled them with a paste of dried raisins, figs, dates, and honey. They called it a "fruit cake."

This was the only day in the week when the family ate after sunset, and afterwards, just sat around and talked. It was the only evening when Joseph was not to be seen at work on some whittling. Usually he was making handles for tools, but on the Sabbath evening everyone rested in the light of the Sabbath lamp. Like an angel of God, the holy day atmosphere had entered the house and taken possession of it. When, after evening prayer, Jesus went to bed, his little heart was full of joy, looking forward to the next morning.

At last the eagerly-awaited day dawned. After morning prayer on the Sabbath, there was an ample meal, bread and milk, and dried fruit, and butter and honey with the bread. Then Jesus walked between mother and father to the synagogue.

The narrow streets were all swept clean and

seemed wider and much neater. The bazaars everywhere were closed. It was all very quiet and solemn.

The synagogue was a larger building than their simple homes. It had an anteroom containing great pitchers of water, where all poured water over their hands. As they entered the synagogue, Mary went to a place reserved for the women behind a wooden grille, while Jesus sat down next to his father. In front of them was a stage-like platform on which stood a reading desk, in front of a great curtain. Jesus knew that behind that curtain were kept the sacred scrolls of Holy Scripture. Before the reading desk was a bench on which all the important men of Nazareth sat, facing the people.

When the whole congregation had assembled, the precentor of the synagogue gave a sign to the sexton, who signalled the cantor to begin. All arose, and those in the bench on the platform had to turn around so that everyone would be facing the Temple in Jerusalem. Then the whole congregation, in unison, would solemnly recite the *Sh'ma*. Next the precentor, whose head was veiled, offered in the name of all present, not all of the "Eighteen Benedictions" of weekdays, but only the first three and the last three. After each one all would respond, "Amen." Before the last prayer, however, he would turn to them, lift up his hands, and pronounce the blessing of Aaron:

> "The Lord bless you and keep you;
> The Lord show you His face
> And have mercy on you.
> The Lord turn His countenance to you
> And give you peace."

Then all sat down for the chief part of the service, the reading of the Holy Scriptures from the reading desk. One reading was given from the Prophets and seven from the Law. Readers were notified beforehand so that they could prepare themselves. Men or boys could be chosen. How Jesus looked forward to the day when he, too, might be included. He looked at the readers hoping and wishing to stand there one day.

Every reader went to the place designated and unrolled the manuscript. The scrolls were rolled in from the left and from the right, and had to be unrolled accordingly. The reader read in Hebrew. Next to him sat one of the elders, well-versed in the Scriptures. He translated into the Aramaic vernacular. When the readings were over, one of the elders gave a sermon.

The reader from the Prophets could choose to his own liking any passage from any Prophet, but the readers of the Law had no choice. Each one took up where the preceding one left off. Within three years they were supposed to have read the books of the Law once. After the sermon, the congregation was dismissed with a blessing.

Outside the synagogue Joseph and Jesus waited for Mary. On the way home they would sometimes make little detours, watching out, however, never to exceed the two thousand paces allowed for the Sabbath (about five-eighths of a mile).

During the week, when women met at the well, or were gathering firewood in the afternoon, Mary might hear that someone was ill. Jesus knew then that there would be a visit to the sick person on the Sabbath. When they had returned from the synagogue and had finished their second meal, the mother would say: "Shall we go and see how so and so is feeling today?" She always took Jesus with her on those visits to the sick. Mary had great compassion for anyone who was suffering, nor did she ever come with empty hands. She always had Jesus carry a basket with oil and wine, dried fruit and some of their fruitcake. Even as a small boy he felt what a great consolation went out from his mother when she bent over the sick person with the greeting, *Shalom*.

What Mary did for the sick, she also did for the poor. Although her home was very simple, with just enough to meet their needs, they had everything necessary and were never destitute. Others were much poorer than they, and when Mary heard of a case of real poverty and starvation, she always found an extra garment in her chest, and some food to spare. Always she was busy spinning and weaving to produce something extra, to have something to give to others.

After the little Sabbath walk, they returned to the synagogue for the afternoon service. There was another Scripture reading, usually continued from the one in the morning, but without the solemn liturgical ceremonies.

Then it was time to go home for the evening meal which must be finished before the appearance of the evening star which terminated the holy day. Again Mary set the table, either in the courtyard or in the room, and decked it with all the delicacies she had prepared. Again the three gathered around it on the floor and, after saying grace, enjoyed the good meal. If Joseph had not accompanied them on the visit, he spoke during supper of what he had done. Sometimes friends or relatives had come to visit him and discuss the topics of the time: the latest outrages of the Romans, the increased prices because of heavy taxation, the impatient awaiting of the Messiah to come.

Nevertheless the day was always filled with holiness and peace, a day of rest for the greater honor and glory of God.

4

THE HOUSE OF JAHWEH

The most beautiful hours for the son of Mary were the quiet evenings of story-telling, when his mother would talk to him of her years in the Temple. Schools for girls did not exist since the rabbis feared that domestic duties would suffer if women spent time in study. Mary, however, coming from one of the highest families in the land, had been eligible to become a Temple virgin and to receive the best education from learned rabbis and scribes. The maidens in the Temple also learned all a woman's domestic duties. They were taught to cook and wash, to spin and to weave, to embroider and to sing, as well as how to read and write.

Over and over, from the time Jesus was old enough to understand, Mary had described for him the Temple, the one place in which sacrifices could be offered to God, the only house of Jahweh on earth. Closing his eyes, he could picture the tremendous piles of stonework towering high over the city of Jerusalem, with Herod's thousands of builders climbing like tiny ants from stone to stone. He could see the pure gold of the great Holy House gleaming and sparkling in the sun, the vast courts and cloisters and colonnades with their brilliantly-colored marbles, the massive gold and silver of the great gates.

With each retelling, Jesus was drawn closer and closer to the Holy City he had not yet seen. Step by step, in the story, he and his mother would make the pilgrimage. Together they would pause on Mount Olivet. They followed the winding road down into the valley and across the brook Kidron (Cedron). They set their faces for the last steep climb "up to Jerusalem"—up, up, and then suddenly they had come through the gate and were in the great Court of the Gentiles beneath the mighty columns of the Royal Porch. From the eastern corner of the wall behind them, they could look down to the bottom of the Kidron Valley, and it was of a steepness to make one giddy. Yet in front of them the House of God, the Temple itself towered loftily over all.

Mary's story always took them next to the Court of the Women, where, as a cloistered maiden, she had gone daily, for the sacred ceremonies of the sacrifice. Eagerly her son made her tell it all over again from the beginning. How during the night the Temple gates were closed and the massive keys guarded under a marble slab, while the whole vast enclosure was wrapped in silence and darkness; how, long before dawn priests and Levites were busy with preparations for the day's sacrifice, which was always a yearling lamb without blemish, an offering of incense, and twelve loaves. Jesus knew that to be a priest of the Temple one must descend from Aaron, but that sons of Levi, the Levites, were also in the Temple as helpers, for as Mary had told him in the words of the Scriptures, "Then Moses stood in the gate of the camp, and said, 'Whoever is for the Lord, come to me' and all the sons of Levi gathered together to him" (Exodus 32:26).

When lots had been cast for the first duties of the day, one priest was sent to the pinnacle of the Temple to watch for the dawn. When the Temple maidens arose Mount Olivet in the east was still a silhouette against the gray sky. Together they turned their faces toward the House of Gold and solemnly recited the "Eighteen Benedictions," which one day Mary was to teach her son:

"O Lord, open Thou my lips
And my mouth shall declare thy praise.
Blessed art Thou, O Lord, our God and

39

God of our Fathers,

God of Abraham, God of Isaac, God of Jacob,

The great, mighty, and revered God,

The most high God who bestoweth loving kindness

And possesseth all things,

Who rememberest the pious deed of the patriarchs

And in love wilt bring a Redeemer to their children's children

For Thy Name's sake."

Then suddenly from behind the hill across the valley came the first ray of sun, and with the watchman's long, loud, drawn-out hail, "The—morning—shineth!" The answering call rose from below: "Is the sky bright as far as Hebron?"

Now the gray of the sky went quickly, and there were glimpses of white in the green valley. Once again the watchman's voice sounded, "The sky is lit up as far as Hebron!"

Instantly, all silence was shattered. The presiding priest lifted his powerful voice and sent out his command: "Priests, to your duties!" "Levites, to your chants!" "Israelites, to your places!"

At this moment the Levites opened the great gates, everyone took his appointed station, and the faithful began to flock into the outer courts.

The Temple maidens watched the sacred ceremonies from behind a latticed gallery in the open Court of the Women. As Mary described it so vividly it seemed to her son that he too was peering through the lattice, past the gigantic eastern gate, to catch a glimpse of the huge altar of holocaust, where a triple fire was blazing and great clouds of incense were rising to the sky. Now the lamb was fetched out and given its last drink of a golden bowl. Ninety-three priests took their places. As the silver trumpets sounded a triple signal, the lamb's throat was cut and the blood caught in gold and silver vessels. They could see the white gowns of the priests turn red with the blood as the lamb was cut, skinned, and offered, and behind it all, the beautiful Golden House, Jahweh's abode on earth.

Next there would be a tense moment as the second lot was cast, to decide which priest might have the honor of offering incense. There was a deep, waiting silence. Suddenly, a dense column of fragrant smoke came curling out through the windows and rising high in the air above the golden roof of the Holy House. All the watching faithful fell prostrate in adoration and prayed to God to bless his people and to send his Holy One within their own days.

"Magnified and sanctified be His great Name," were the words of the *Kaddish*, "in the world which He has created according to His will.

May He establish His kingdom in your life and during your days, and during the life of the whole household of Israel, even speedily, and in the near time, so be it. Amen."

Meanwhile parts of the lamb had been brought to the altar of holocausts and arranged in the fire. The drink offering was poured out at the base of the altar and twelve half loaves thrown into the flame. Then, all the priests together, standing on the steps, raised their arms shoulder high and recited together the solemn blessing which had been given to the people in the desert: "The Lord bless you, and keep you; the Lord make His face shine on you, and be gracious to you; the Lord lift up His countenance on you, and give you peace" (Numbers 6:24-26).

After the blessing, everyone rose to the singing of the psalm of the day. Choir, stringed-instruments, and silver trumpets together made such loud and festive music that it could be heard all over the city. When the last chord had died away, the morning sacrifice was over.

There in the courts of the Temple, Mary passed her childhood. Day after day she had listened to the mighty sound of the Temple drum, the *Magrepha*, and had seen the priests hands raised in blessing over the prostrate people.

Her son could not hear enough about those years, or about the glory and majesty of the House of God on earth. Over and over he listened to her tell of it, waiting most impatiently and eagerly for the time when he would be taken along with his mother and father, on the annual pilgrimage to Jerusalem. Each time he begged for the story of her years as a Temple virgin. His longing to see the House of the Lord grew, especially when He heard her exclaim in the words of their ancestor, David, "I have loved, O Lord, the beauty of Thy house, and the place where Thy glory dwelleth" (Psalm 26:8).

5

THE FEAST OF FEASTS

Jesus did not have to wait long for the first family pilgrimage to the Holy City. According to the rabbis' decree, a child might partake in the celebration of the holy *Pasch* as soon as he could eat meat.

So one spring day his cousins began telling him of the wonderful trip ahead, in which he would share this time. On all sides preparations were being made for the pilgrimage. Men were busy repairing the roads, fixing bridges, and white-washing the sepulchres along the roadside. In the homes women were getting the clothes ready; and in the synagogues special prayers were added in preparation for the great feast. The children were most expectant, eagerly looking forward to the great treat in store for them. Jesus was too young to ask the full meaning of it all, but his small heart could feel the deep religious and patriotic emotions which were aroused everywhere.

Finally the day of departure arrived. All the people from Nazareth went in a group . . . the better to ward off robbers and wild animals. While most of them walked on foot, families with little children used donkeys. Joseph had a donkey which helped him transport heavy beams from the lumberyard to the places where they were needed on new homes. He had made a little chair, attached to the donkey's saddle, for Jesus.

As Jesus rode, he looked around eagerly. A few of the rich people had camels, and one of the very wealthy ones could afford a chariot. All those on foot had a staff in hand, water skins and food baskets hanging from their shoulders. The people had elected a leader of the pilgrimage, and when everybody was ready, he called out: "Arise ye and let us go up to Zion unto the Lord, our God." Whereupon the cantor of the synagogue would entone, "How lovely are thy tabernacles, O Lord of hosts." And everyone would join in, "My soul longeth and fainteth for the courts of the Lord. My heart and my flesh have rejoiced in the living God."

Nazareth lies about 85 miles north of Jerusalem. It took them four and one-half days to make the pilgrimage. Nights were spent at one of the many inns by the roadside. Such an inn, or *Khan* consisted of a large walled-in area. The walls were fifteen feet high and were a protection during the night against robbers, lions, wolves and jackals.

In the middle of the inn grounds, the innkeeper kindled a large fire where the pilgrims could warm themselves before lying down on the sleeping mats which they had brought along, covering themselves with heavy camel's-hair coats. Some of the pilgrims took sacrificial animals along from home, while others would buy them at the Temple market. Such an inn was a place teeming with men, women, children— camels and donkeys, cattle and lambs.

After morning prayers, with faces turned toward the Holy City they were approaching, they ate dried fruit and drank water from their skins. Even on the trip, people had already banded together in groups of families and friends, as the Law prescribed that the *Pasch* should be eaten in groups of not less than twelve, not more than twenty.

The mothers of the group would avail themselves of the large mills and baking ovens made ready by the innkeeper to bake the daily supply of bread from the grain they had brought from home. Soon after six o'clock they would be on the road again. One stop would be made for the noonday meal consisting of dried fruit, bread and cheese, water or milk. The evening meal would be cooked in the next *Khan*—a stew of lentils or beans with plenty of bread. There was a joyous air about the whole group. Though tired after a long day's march, they were happily tired.

As they walked on, passing through hamlets and small towns, other pilgrims would join them until, on the last day, the road would be covered with an unbroken line of people and animals. It was a long procession. Most of the time the travelers would sing hymns and psalms. On the final stage of the trip, pipers led with their instruments. With each day the enthusiasm of the pilgrims kept mounting.

On the last morning Jesus' cousins kept telling him that soon now they would see the Holy City. And, as they followed once more around a curve in the road, there it was just as his mother had described it to him, Jerusalem the beautiful, with its massive walls and many towers, and the glorious Temple building surrounding them. The Golden House—sparkling in the sun! For a moment all noise stopped. A reverent hush fell over the whole large group, until the instruments started again and everyone joined in the singing of the One Hundred Twenty-second Psalm: "I was glad when they said to me, 'Let us go to the house of the Lord. . . . Pray for the peace of Jerusalem: May they prosper who love you.' "

At the city gate, representatives of Jerusalem greeted the pilgrims. There were rulers and treasurers of the Temple, harpists and choristers with their instruments who said, "Brethren, men of Nazareth, you are welcome!"

They entered the city by the Garden Gate and went first to the place assigned to them, where they were to spend the seven days of the feast.

Jerusalem was bigger—much bigger, than Mary's description had led Jesus to imagine. Everywhere people were coming and going, and the whole vast enclosure seemed to be alive with animals—lowing oxen and hundreds and hundreds of lambs bleating under the burning sun, while pilgrims bartered and bargained, and money-changers shouted and counted their ill-gotten coins.

Mary and Joseph looked sad as they hastened by such noisy, dishonest groups. They worked their way across the great courtyard and around the *Sorag*, a low screen of marble pillars, to the eastern side of the inner wall. Mount Olivet and Gethsemane were behind them, as they mounted the fourteen steps, crossed a broad platform, they now stood before the Beautiful Gate, the main entrance to the Temple.

First came the Court of the Women. Up a flight of marble steps, flashed the gleaming gold and silver of the Nicanor Gate, beyond which

Jesus knew were the great altar of holocausts and the Temple itself. Mary remained in the Court of the Women as Joseph and Jesus proceeded up the steps and into the "Court of Israel."

Before them, in the Court of the Priests, stood the great altar of holocausts with its tremendous bulk of unhewn stone, and below it the Brazen Laver, a huge flower-shaped bowl resting on twelve brass bulls. They could see in the marble floor the rings to which sacrificial animals would be tied. On a great silver table, the gold and silver vessels of the sacrifice gleamed in the sun; and on the table of the altar itself, three fires burned steadily.

It was forbidden to enter the Temple with sandals, bags and staff, or dust on one's feet, so their sandals and all travelling equipment were left outside. The leader of the pilgrimage cautioned them that even in front of the gates reverence and respect were to be shown.

In a whisper, Joseph pointed out the entrance to the Holy House and the veil of four colors behind which dwelt the Living God. Deep joy and holy awe flooded the heart of Jesus. From then on he was always to feel homesick away from the Temple.

Jesus had an uncle by the name of Zacharias who was from the tribe of Aaron and was a priest for the Temple. He and his wife, Elizabeth, lived in Ain-Karim, only a short distance outside of Jerusalem in the hills, but he had also a house in the city. As long as the old couple lived, Mary, Joseph and Jesus were most probably invited to spend the Holy Week with them in Jerusalem. They had only one son, John, whom Jesus had never met. During one stay in their home, he overheard his aunt telling his mother that the young boy had gone away into the wilderness to lead the strict life of a hermit.

Zacharias also invited friends from the near-by village of Bethany. They had three children: a boy, Lazarus; and two girls, Martha and Mary. They were usually members of the group celebrating the *Pasch* together.

The Passover was always held on the same day, the fourteenth of the month Nisan (April). On the preceding evening, the thirteenth of the month Nisan, everyone met in the dining room. Then Uncle Zacharias, head of the house, appeared with a lighted candle, and as all faced toward the Temple, he prayed: "Blessed art Thou, Jahweh, our God, King of the universe, who hast sanctified us by Thy commandments and commanded us to remove the leaven."

Next he searched with candle into every corner of the room, especially in all places where leaven was usually kept. Of course, the women had removed it all earlier. This was only a ceremonious search, after which he prayed again: "All the leaven that is in my possession, that

51

which I have seen and that which I have not seen, be it null, be it counted as the dust of the earth."

This search was accomplished in perfect silence. For seven days the only bread to be used was unleavened loaves. The boy Jesus was deeply touched by the search for the leaven.

The feast for which they all had come to Jerusalem was really threefold: the *Pasch*, the Feast of the Unleavened Bread, and the Feast of the First Fruit.

The next day, the fourteenth of Nisan, was the holiest day of the seven. From noon on, no work was done; the whole city took on a festive air.

Early in the morning the fathers, who were responsible for the eating of the Paschal lamb, went out to select the proper animal, one without blemish, not more than one year, not less than eight days, old.

During their first few Passovers Joseph went alone for the Paschal lamb, slaughtered it in the Temple, offered its blood, had it skinned and brought it to his uncle's home, while Jesus stayed with his mother who helped his aunt with the preparations for the solemn meal at night.

His uncle was saddened that people at this time were beginning to forget many of the old customs. He, himself, was very strict. In the entrance hall to the dining room he kept special mantles, staffs and wide-brimmed hats ready for all participants; and, as each entered the room, he was handed his set by a servant. Then all stood around a longish table with Zacharias presiding, and they were told to eat and drink in haste according to the word of Moses: "And thus you shall eat it; you shall gird your loins and you shall have shoes on your feet, and holding staves in your hands and you shall eat it in haste, for it is the *Phase* (that is, the passage) of the Lord."

One of the exciting things of this night for the small children was that they were allowed to stay up long beyond their usual time. The solemn meal started around nine o'clock in the evening. It began with a cup of wine mixed with water. Then all washed their right hands again, took some of the lettuce, dipped it in a tart sauce, and ate it.

Next Zacharias pronounced solemnly the blessing over the lamb: "Blessed is He Who sanctifies us with His Commandments and ordered us to eat the Passover."

The Paschal lamb was brought in, and the bitter herbs were dipped and eaten together with the meat of the lamb. Next the second cup of wine was served. That was the moment when everyone looked at the son of Mary and Joseph. He was the youngest first-born boy at the table, and as such had the right to ask the question of the evening:

"Why is this night different from other nights? For on all other nights we eat leavened bread, but on this night only unleavened bread? On all other nights we eat any kind of herbs, but on this night only bitter herbs? On all other nights we eat meat stewed or boiled, but on this night only roasted? On all other nights we dip the herbs only once, but on this night twice?

Jesus had been memorizing this long question weeks ahead of time, and now he was happy when he could see in the eyes of his mother and father that he had said it well.

In answer to the question, Zacharias instructed them all, while addressing himself to the boy about the importance of the night. He began with their people's disgrace in Egypt, ending with their future glory. He gave a learned discourse about their whole national history and explained each small detail. Then more cups of wine were served, four in all, each preceded by another washing of hands; and during all that time the great "*Hallel* Psalms" were sung by the family group. After one last benediction, the father of the house dismissed them. In the anteroom they took off their liturgical garments, and in solemn silence, everyone withdrew to go to sleep. High in the sky the big bright moon, the full moon of spring, shed its light on this holy night.

The next day, or the fifteenth of Nisan, was

called "the first day of the unleavened bread." It was still a holiday with no unnecessary work done, and all went to the morning sacrifice and to the Temple. After the public sacrifice for the whole nation was offered, the private offerings of each individual were brought. On the next day was the Feast of the First Fruit. In the evening (all days started in the evening, instead of morning) just as the sun went down, three men, each with a sickle and basket, went to a place which was marked out by the elders where the new barley was to be cut. A whole procession went with these men and they asked of the bystanders four questions:

"Has the sun gone down?"

The people would answer, "Yes."

"Should we reap with this sickle?"

The people answering, "Yes."

"Into this basket?"

"Yes."

And finally, "Shall I reap?"

The people again responded: "Thou shalt reap."

They then cut down ceremoniously a bushel of the new barley. The ears were brought into the court of the Temple to be threshed with flails, then parched on a perforated pan over the holy fire, and exposed for the wind. The grain thus prepared was ground in a barley mill. The flour was passed through many sieves, each one finer than the other, until it was fine enough to be offered in the Temple. Mixed with oil and frankincense, it was waved before the Lord. A handful was taken out and burned before the altar; the remainder belonged to the priests. That was called the "Presentation of the First Fruit," on the second day of the Passover Feast on the sixteenth of Nisan.

The next days were minor feast days. All work was allowed again. The last day of the Passover, the twenty-first of Nisan, was a great holiday again and observed like a Sabbath.

Year after year Jesus came to Jerusalem with his mother and father, fulfilling the duty imposed on him by the ancient Law and customs of his people. Each year he understood more of the holy ceremony and penetrated more deeply into the liturgical meaning of this memorial feast of the redemption of Israel.

As a little boy he had greatly enjoyed spending part of the day roaming around with cousins and friends through the fabulous bazaars of Jerusalem; but as he grew older, he no longer felt drawn to these childish pastimes. He wanted to "dwell in the courts of the Lord," as had his ancestor, David.

More and more, too, he saw that their Feast of the Passover had a twofold meaning: it was a memorial of the great things God had done for his people in the past, but it was also a symbol of things to come when, in a much greater Passover than the ones they were then celebrating, He would redeem his people from their sins.

6

THE SON OF JOSEPH THE CARPENTER

When Joseph Ben-David began to teach Jesus the entire *Sh'ma* and the Psalms of the *Hallel* (Psalms 112-117), Jesus stopped being a *Taph*. He was now an *Elem*, and shortly after his sixth year, with other boys of his age, began to go to school. There was an elementary school attached to every synagogue, and from the age of five, boys were sent there to learn the Law and to read the *Torah*, the five books of Moses, known as the *Pentateuch*.

Such schools were very austere. The morning session began at six and lasted for four hours in the summer, a little longer in winter. Jesus went home for the morning meal, as did the others. In the afternoon, all returned to school and stayed until supper, though on feast days and fast days the hours were somewhat shorter.

The boys wore tunics and cloaks, the older ones also having a covering for their heads. At all times they sat on the floor in a respectful group with their teacher. Each brought with him a wax tablet, a stylus and a small parchment roll of the Law. Moses had said: "These words, which I command thee this day, shall be in thy heart, and thou shalt tell them to thy children." This was taken literally. It was the custom to begin with the book *Leviticus*, then follow with the other four books and, after that, the Prophets and other sacred writings.

Besides learning to read Hebrew, the boys were also instructed in the meaning of the holy texts. All their knowledge and wisdom came from the Scriptures which also served as textbooks for history, geography, and philosophy.

Once the boys had started going to school, they separated from the girls and played alone in their free time. They would climb the hills behind Nazareth, and loved to watch vinedressers in the vineyards at the time of harvest, or the sowers scattering seed in the early rainy season. They saw the grain winnowed and harvested, and during the threshing they followed the oxen round and round their turning circle.

While the boy Jesus, now an *Elem*, still helped his mother to carry water and collect firewood, the free hours when he had watched her weaving or spinning were now spent in another way. He was in Joseph's workshop, becoming an apprentice.

This apprenticeship would last for ten years. At first the father merely showed him how to hold tools, how to plane, how to use a chisel and to wedge two boards. School took most of the morning and afternoon hours, so what he learned in Joseph's workshop was usually by watching.

As he watched, his admiration, love and respect grew steadily for the young man who was such a loving father. Joseph, the carpenter, was truly of royal blood with his tall, youthful figure and bronzed complexion, with his brilliant eyes, regular features, and strong but slender hands and feet. His grave dignity of speech and manner impressed all the neighbors, who were well aware of exalted birth and, when availing themselves of his services as carpenter would respectfully address him by his title: Joseph Ben-David— Joseph, son of David.

He was also a skilled artisan and an independent tradesman, a combination of cabinetmaker, carpenter and builder, a "just man" who worked zealously that his wife and son might suffer no want. The work of a carpenter was always in demand, especially since King Herod kept 15,000 men at work on the Temple in Jerusalem and had drained the countryside of nearly all skilled labor. Young and capable craftsmen like Joseph, who did not want to work for Herod, were much sought after and had always more business than they could handle.

Theirs was a quiet house. If Mary was not given to many words, Joseph was still more silent. As Joseph and Jesus worked side by side in the shop or courtyard, time would pass without a word. Joseph would beckon when he wanted to show something to his son. He would nod if the boy worked well, or smilingly shake his head and show him again. He would always listen gravely to the talkative neighbors, saying what he wanted to say in a very few words. Only when he explained the Law to Jesus would he become eloquent. His eyes shone and his youthful face glowed with an inner light when he talked about the mercy of God toward his people.

Joseph had only one wish: to purchase all of the holy books. These hand-copied scrolls were very expensive, but patiently he added coin to coin until he could afford yet another. Then he would come home from the market, showing happily his newest treasure and reading to his family in the evenings, or on the Sabbath.

He would read about their ancestors, the illustrious kings David, Solomon, Hezekiah and Josiah; or the wicked ones, Uzziah and Manasseh; famous men like Boaz and Zerubbabel; or women of such diverse fame as Rahab, Ruth and Bathsheba.

The humble Joseph was nevertheless most proud to point out that he and his wife were both of royal blood. He would explain to Jesus that the most famous rabbi of their time, Hillel, who was also descended from David, was nevertheless of inferior birth because his lineage went back, not through the kings to Solomon, the son of David and Bathsheba, but to Abigail, the mischosen wife of David, who was not the mother of any of his royal successors.

Up to his twelfth year Jesus was called "son of Joseph," but his father always pointed out that when he became of age he would inherit his official title of royalty and from then on be called "Jesus, son of David."

The family of David was respected as the first family in the land because all people knew that someday the Messiah was to be born from among them.

7

"PRAISE THE LORD WITH CYMBALS"

Three times a year the Jewish people were supposed to go to the Holy Place in Jerusalem. (Those who were more than a day's journey away were not strictly obliged.) God had sent word through the lawgiver, Moses, that at certain intervals they should pause to lift up their hearts and minds to God and to commemorate the great things He had done for them.

On the fifteenth of Nisan God gathered his people around the sanctuary for the solemn Feast of *Pasch*. This time they were to come with a grateful heart and recall how He had helped them against their mighty enemy, the Pharaoh of Egypt, and had led out His beloved people from captivity into the freedom of the children of God.

On the Feast of Weeks, or Pentecost, was celebrated the anniversary of the giving of the Law on Mt. Sinai.

Once more God called His children to the most joyous of the festive seasons in all Israel, the Feast of Tabernacles. It fell at the time of the year when the hearts of the people were naturally full of gratefulness and gladness, late in the fall, when all of the crops had been stored, all the fruits had been harvested and the land was expecting the refreshment of the rains to prepare it for a new crop.

These were the three major feasts given to the chosen people by Moses fourteen hundred years before the time of Jesus. Each feast lasted for a week, and every man was to come to Jerusalem for these times, if he could possibly do so.

Besides these great feasts, there were a number of smaller festivals like the Feast of Purim, celebrating the events told in the Book of Esther, when the Jews were delivered from the Persians. This occurred in the month Adar (March) on the fourteenth day.

The Feast of Lights—Hanukah—was observed on the twenty-fifth of the month of Chislev (a pious tradition makes it December 25), and was instituted by the great countrymen of Jesus, the Maccabees, to commemorate the restoration of worship at the Temple after it had been desecrated by the Gentiles. The first new grapes of the year were eaten at this festival.

The "Day of Atonement," *Yom Kippur*, often called simply the "Day of Days," falls on the tenth day of the seventh month (October). That included a most touching ceremony in which the High Priest sent the scapegoat away into the wilderness laden with the people's sins.

Every week had its feast day on the Sabbath, so every month had its festive season on the "day of the new moon," which marked the beginning of each new month. Special priests were on duty to watch for the showing of the new moon, and would announce it to the nation by blowing silver trumpets from the pinnacle of the Temple. Instantly, fires would be lit on the Mount of Olives and observed from the neighboring hills. In no time the news spread throughout the country. The words of the priest, "It is sanctified," were intended to give a hallowed character to each month. This was always a very popular feast. Quite distinct from the other new moons, and more sacred, was that of the seventh month, or "Tishri," as it was called, which marked the commencement of the civil year—New Year's Day. This was known as "the Day of Blowing" because on that day the trumpets were blown all day long in Jerusalem. The new moon of the seventh month was to be observed as a Sabbath day and special offerings were ordained for it.

With the liturgical year and the civil year, there were also two New Year's Days. Besides the civil New Year's Day, all celebrated a liturgical New Year's Day which was on the first day of Elul (the sixth month). All flocks and herds were tithed, and the rabbis said that all the children of men passed before Jahweh like lambs on this day, as it is written: "He fashioneth their hearts alike, He considereth all their works."

The ordinary happenings of family life were also elevated and given a festive character. Birth, marriage and death are the great occurrences in every family the world over. But they did not simply "occur" for the people of Israel they were celebrated as major feasts with an octave, like the major feasts of the Lord.

When a baby was born into a Jewish home, all the children of the neighborhood rejoiced because they knew that a week after the birthday would be the feast of name-giving. If it were a boy, it would be circumcision; if it were a girl, it would be a slightly less solemn ritual. But in either case, all the children of the neighborhood were invited by the parents, who showed the new baby to the children and gave a children's party with cakes and drink and games. How many times as a little boy Jesus was invited to such joyful parties in Nazareth!

The greatest event in a family, however, was a marriage feast. Mary was frequently asked to come and take part in the preparations of the different marriages in their large family. The women would start two weeks before with baking, and roasting, smoking fish and meat, ordering and arranging. The bridegroom would appoint his best friend to distribute the invitations.

A year before the wedding feast they would have already celebrated the feast of betrothal which took place before two witnesses, where they exchanged a ring. The rabbi asked them certain questions and gave them his blessing. After this betrothal, the two persons were regarded as belonging to each other, almost as if they were already married. In that year the bride worked busily on her dowry.

Then came the great day.

On the evening of the wedding feast the bridegroom would come with all his friends to take his bride home. Such a wedding procession could be heard throughout the whole town— there was so much shouting, singing and flute-playing going on. All the people in the bridegroom's party carried torches, while the bride and bridesmaids were waiting with lighted lamps in their hands. The moment of marriage took place when the bridegroom guided his bride over the threshold of her new home. That made her his wife. Afterwards, the solemn marriage meal took place. The newly-wed pair sat under a canopy on a kind of throne in special fine clothing. The meal was always lavish.

Many times Mary told her son how people went into heavy debt to make that day the greatest of their lives. When Jesus used to accompany Mary to the well to help her draw the daily supply of water, he could hear the women chatter for weeks after a wedding about the crown of the bride, her jewels, and her bridal garment.

Even a funeral had its festive character. There always had to be witnesses around a dying person. As soon as the spirit had left the body, the eyes and mouth of the corpse were closed by the nearest of kin. The body was then washed, anointed and clothed in a white garment. Then it was laid out and the near relatives started to lament loudly. Finally, the professional wailers arrived. They tore their hair, sometimes they even lacerated their cheeks, rent their clothes, cast ashes upon their heads and shrieked loud lamentations.

The burial had to take place within twenty-four hours. The corpse was bound up for the grave and a special piece of linen was spread over the face. Then the body was placed upon a simple bier and was buried either in the ground, or in a cave. In the latter case, a heavy stone was needed to close the entrance against wild animals. For several weeks afterwards relatives would wear clothes of mourning.

Besides the celebration of all these feasts, the people of Israel observed a great many folk customs and traditions handed down from generation to generation. Like every other Jewish child, Jesus learned to know them. He was told, for instance, that bread must never be cut with a knife, that it mighty only be broken. Though friends in other parts of the world went arm-in-arm, Jesus' people went hand-in-hand. If a dear friend took his leave to go on a journey, they used to drink the cup of friendship on the eve of his departure. It was a little informal gathering of all the friends who broke bread and drank wine as a sign of friendship with the one who was about to depart, as a token that they would never forget each other.

People from towns which were further than one day's journey away from Jerusalem were not strictly obliged to attend the major feasts at the Temple. They could celebrate in their local synagogue. This would have been the case for Joseph and his family, as it took them over four days to get to the Holy City.

To miss nine work days is something to consider for every artisan, but Joseph always thought that God cannot be outdone in generosity—that God would make up in his own good way the time one lost on these pilgrimages three times a year.

As soon as Jesus was grown up, he accompanied Joseph and his mother not only for the Passover, but also for the Feast of Pentecost and Tabernacles.

Jesus noticed that the attendance at the Temple for the other two feasts was not quite as large as at the Passover, yet the Temple area was always crowded. Pentecost began on the evening of the fiftieth day after Passover. During the first watch (between nine o'clock and midnight) the great altar of holocausts was cleansed and, immediately after midnight, the Temple gates were thrown open. Before the morning sacrifice, all the offerings which the people brought to the Temple had to be examined by the priests. For that reason they must all be on duty. Each was kept very busy.

The particular offering of the day was that of the two whey-loaves with their accompanying sacrifices of seven lambs, one young bullock and two rams. In contrast to those of the Feast of Passover, such loaves were made with leaven. Specially fine wheat flour was used and they were baked in the Temple the night before the feast. Each loaf had to be four hands wide, seven long, and four fingers high—and made about five pounds of bread. These loaves represented the ordinary food of the people and were offered in thanksgiving for the daily bread. As at Passover, the first and seventh days of the Feast of

Pentecost were kept as Sabbath, and the days in-between were minor feast days.

The festival that all liked most, however, was the Feast of Tabernacles. Somehow everyone was naturally in a most festive mood with the harvest over and all the work done and the expectations for the early rains. This feast the Jewish people celebrated not in their houses, but in little huts which they made from fresh boughs of trees. There they ate and prayed, studied and slept for a whole week. This practice had been ordained by Jahweh to recall that once His chosen people lived in tents for forty years, while He kept them waiting in the desert.

Families vied with each other to have the nicest hut. There were special regulations: the huts must be high enough, yet not too high, at least ten hands, but not more than thirty hands; three of the walls must be made of boughs; they must be fairly covered, yet had to admit sunshine.

In the Temple there were special offerings. Again, as at the Passover and at Pentecost, the altar of holocausts was cleansed during the first night watch, and the gates of the Temple were thrown open immediately after midnight, when the offerings of the faithful were inspected. Just before the morning service began, a priest, accompanied by a joyous procession with music, went down to the Pool of Siloam where he blew a small amount of water into a golden pitcher. While one procession went for the water of Siloam, another brought willow branches from the Valley of Kidron. These were secured on either side of the altar midst the blast of the priests' trumpets, and were then bent over the altar to form a kind of canopy.

The ordinary morning sacrifice proceeded. The priest, who had gone with his procession to Siloam had to time his return for the exact moment when his brethren carried up the pieces of the sacrificial animals to lay them on the altar. As the procession entered by the Water Gate, which derives its name from this ceremony, they were received by a threefold blast from silver trumpets. The priest went up to the altar with the water and turned to the left. There he found two silver basins with narrow holes. Into these the wine of the drink offering was poured and, at the same time, the water from Siloam. At the moment when wine and water were being poured out, the Temple music began, the singing and playing of the great "*Hallel* Psalms." When the choir came to the words, "O, give thanks to the Lord," all worshippers waved their branches toward the altar, in accordance with the words of the Prophet, "You shall draw waters with joy out of the Saviour's fountains." With these ceremonies prayers were offered for the much-needed rains.

Every day, at the end of the morning sacrifice, the priests formed a procession and made the circuit of the altar, singing, "Oh, then, now work salvation, Jahweh. O, Jahweh, give prosperity."

And on the last day of the feast, the so-called "Great Day," they made a circuit of the altar seven times, remembering how the walls of Jericho had fallen, and praying that similarly the walls of paganism would fall before Jahweh.

These were most joyful days, the "Day of the Great Hosannah," the "Day of the Great Willows," the "Day of the Beating of the Branches," and finally, the "Great Day."

There was one more ceremony connected with this feast, one which made it especially popular. At the close of the first day the worshippers went to the Court of the Women where great preparations had been made. The vestments of the priests which when they were soiled, could not be washed and used again, were torn up and made into wicks for lamps. Then four golden candelabras were prepared, each with four golden bowls. Four young priests filled each bowl with the finest oil and lit the wicks with holy fire from the altar. All the faithful had come with torches or lamps in their hands and received the holy fire which they carried home with them. There was not one court in Jerusalem that was not lit up with holy light, and the whole Temple was illuminated, as a sign that the people "who walk in darkness shall receive the great light."

On the afternoon of the seventh day, the great celebration was over, and the people began to move from their huts back into their homes.

Not for anything would Jesus have missed this feast. Again and again he was deeply moved by the ceremonies of the living water and the holy light.

8

THE SON OF DAVID THE KING

Finally came the day to which each boy of Jesus' age looked forward with most eager longing: the twelfth birthday when he would be declared a "son of the Law."

This was and still is a great day in every Jewish family, known as *Bar Mitzvah*. On the evening of the feast the father would give to his son, together with a solemn blessing, the phylacteries which, from now on, he would be obliged to wear during prayer time, one small box to be fastened around the forehead, and another around the left upper arm. These little boxes contained strips of parchment on which passages of Holy Scripture were written. Then he would give him the *Talith*, a beautifully-woven shawl to be worn over the head during prayer at home, in the synagogue,

77

and in the Temple.

When a boy was initiated into the Law on his twelfth birthday, he had to recite the phylacteries and also from then on, three times a day, the *Shemoneh Esreh*, the "Eighteen Benedictions," the prayers:

1.

Be Thou praised, O Lord,
    our God, the God of
    our fathers,
The God of Abraham, of
    Isaac and Jacob,
The great and mighty and
    dreadful God,
The Supreme Being, dispenser of benefits and
    of favors,
The Creator of all things.
Thou rememberest the
    piety of the patriarchs,
And Thou wilt send a deliverer to their children,
To glorify Thy Name and
    to show forth Thy love.
O King, our help, our
    strength and shield;
Be Thou praised, O Lord,
    the shield of Abraham.

2.

Thou art mighty forever,
O Lord.

Thou causest the wind to
blow and the rain to
descend.

Thou sustainest the living,
Thou quickenest the
dead.

Blessed art Thou, O Lord,
that quickenest the
dead.

3.

Thou art Holy and holy is
Thy Name.

And holy ones praise Thee
every day.

Praised be Thou, O Lord,
the holy God.

4.

Thou givest man wisdom
and fillest him with
understanding.

Praised be Thou, O Lord,
the dispenser of wisdom.

5.

Bring us back to Thy law,

O our Father;

Bring us back, O King, into
Thy service;

Bring us back to Thee by
true repentance.

Praised be Thou, O Lord,
who dost accept our re-
pentance.

6.

Pardon us, O our Father,
for we have sinned.

Pardon us, O our King, for
we have transgressed.

Thou art a God who dost
pardon and forgive.

Praised be Thou, O Lord,
who dost pardon many
times and forever.

7.

Look upon our misery, O
Lord, and be Thou our
defender.

Deliver us speedily for Thy
glory for Thou art the
Almighty Redeemer.

Blessed art Thou, O Lord,
the Redeemer of Israel.

8.

Heal us, O Lord, and we
shall be healed;
Help us and we shall be
helped.
Thou art the One whom
we praise.
Vouchsafe healing to all
our wounds,
Thou art the King Al-
mighty, our true phy-
sician full of mercy!
Blessed art Thou, O Lord,
who healeth the sick of
the children of Thy
people.

9.

Bless us, O Lord, and bless
this year and these
harvests.
Give Thy blessing to the
ground and satisfy us
with Thy goodness,
And make this year one of
the good years.
Blessed art Thou, O Lord,
who blesseth the years.

Sound the trumpet of de-
liverance;
Lift up the standard which
shall gather together the
dispersed of the nation,
And bring us all quickly
back again from the
ends of the earth.
Blessed art Thou, O Lord,
who gathereth Israel.

Restore our judges as in
former times and our
counsellors as in the
beginning,
Deliver us from affliction
and anguish.
Do Thou alone reign over
us by Thy grace and
mercy,
And let not Thy judgment
come upon us.
Blessed art Thou, O Lord,
who loveth truth and
uprightness.

And for slanderers let

there be no hope.

Let all the workers of iniquity and the rebellious be destroyed;

Let the might of the proud be humbled.

Blessed art Thou, O Lord, that humblest the arrogant.

13.

Let Thy mercy, O Lord, be showed upon the upright,

Upon the humble, the elders of Thy people Israel, and the rest of its teachers;

Be favorable to the pious strangers among us and to us all.

Give Thou a good reward to those who sincerely trust in Thy Name,

That our lot may be cast among them in the world to come;

That our hope be not deceived.

Blessed art Thou, O Lord, the trust of the righteous.

14.

Return Thou in Thy mercy
to Thy city Jerusalem.

Make it Thine abode as
Thou hast promised, let
it be built again in our
days.

Let it never be destroyed!

Restore Thou speedily the
throne of David.

Blessed art Thou, O Lord,
who buildest Jerusalem.

15.

Do Thou cause the branch
of David speedily to
flourish,

And make it glorious by
Thy strength for in Thee
do we hope all the day.

Blessed be Thou, O Lord,
who dost make *all things*
glorious.

16.

Hear our voice, O Lord, our
God, and have mercy
upon us.

Hear our prayers in Thy
mercy and loving kind-
ness;

For Thou art the God that
hearest prayer and sup-
plication.

Send us not away, O our
King, until Thou hast
heard us.

Thou dost graciously re-
ceive the prayers of Thy
people Israel.

Praised be Thou, O Lord,
who hearest prayer.

17.

Accept, O Lord, our God,
Thy people Israel,

Restore Thou the service
in the courts of Thy
house.

May our eyes see the day
when Thou in Thy mer-
cy wilt return to Zion.

Praise be Thou, O Lord,
who wilt establish Thy
dwelling place in Zion.

18.

We confess that Thou art
the Lord, our God, and
the God of our fathers
for ever and ever.

Thou art the rock of our
life, the shield of our
salvation from gener-
ation to generation.
Blessing and praise be unto
Thy great and Holy
Name,
For the life which Thou
hast given us;
For our souls which Thou
dost sustain;
For the daily miracles
which Thou dost work
in our behalf;
For the marvelous, loving
kindness with which
Thou dost surround us
at all times—
In the morning, at mid-day
and in the evening.
God of all goodness, Thy
mercy is infinite;
Thy faithfulness fails not—
we hope in Thee forever.
For all these Thy benefits
Thy Name be praised
forever and ever.
Let all that live praise Thee.
Let them praise Thy Name
in sincerity.

Praised be Thou, O Lord,
Thy Name alone is good,
And Thou alone art wor-
thy to be praised.
Give peace and blessing
unto us even unto Israel
Thy people.
Bless us all together, O
Lord, our God.
Blessed art Thou, O Lord,
that blessest with peace.
Amen.

It was a great and solemn moment when, on
the eve of Jesus' twelfth birthday, his father
helped him to put on the phylacteries. His mother
had made the little cases from the hide of a black
calf. The leather strip she had sewn on had a loop
through which passed a thong, one finger wide,
and twenty-four inches long. This was the case for
the arm and it contained one rolled strip of parchment on which the following text was written:

1.

Then the Lord spoke to
Moses, saying, Sanctify to
Me every first-born, the
first offspring of every
womb among the sons of
Israel, both of man and

beast; it belongs to me.

And Moses said to the people, Remember this day in which you went out from Egypt, from the house of slavery; for by a powerful hand the Lord brought you out from this place. And nothing leavened shall be eaten.

On this day in the month of Abib, you are about to go forth. And it shall be when the Lord brings you to the land of the Canaanite, the Hittite, the Amorite, the Hivite and the Jebusite, which He swore to your fathers to give you, a land flowing with milk and honey, that you shall observe this rite in this month.

For seven days you shall eat unleavened bread, and on the seventh day there shall be a feast to the Lord. Unleavened bread shall be eaten throughout the seven days; and nothing leavened shall be seen among you, nor shall any leaven be seen among you in all your borders.

And you shall tell your son on that day, saying, It is because of what the Lord did for me when I came out of Egypt. And it shall serve as a sign to you on your hand, and as a reminder on your forehead, that the law of the Lord may be in your mouth; for with a powerful hand the Lord brought you out of Egypt. Therefore, you shall keep this ordinance at its appointed time from year to year (Exodus 13:1-10).

2.

Now it shall come about when the Lord brings you to the land of the Canaanite, as He swore to you and to your fathers, and gives it to you, that you shall devote to the Lord the first offspring of every womb, and the first offspring of every beast that you own; the males belong to the Lord.

But every first offspring of a donkey you shall redeem with a lamb, but if you do not redeem it, then you shall break its neck; and every first-born of man among your sons you shall redeem. And it shall be when your son asks you in time to come, saying What is this? then you shall say to him, With a powerful hand the Lord brought us out of Egypt, from the house of slavery. And it came about, when Pharaoh was stubborn about letting us go, that the Lord killed every first-born of beast. Therefore, I sacrifice to the Lord the males, the first offspring of every womb, but every first-born of my sons I redeem. So it shall serve as a sign on your hand, and as phylacteries

on your forehead, for with
a powerful hand the Lord
brought us out of Egypt
(Exodus 13:11-16).

3.

Hear, O Israel! The Lord
is our God, the Lord is one!
And you shall love the Lord
your God with all your
heart and with all your soul
and with all your might.

And these words, which
I am commanding you to-
day, shall be on your heart:
and you shall teach them
diligently to your sons and
shall talk of them when
you sit in your house and
when you walk by the way
and when you lie down
and when you rise up.

And you shall bind
them as a sign on your
hand and they shall be as
frontals on your forehead.
And you shall write them
on the doorposts of your
house and on your gates
(Deuteronomy 6:4-9).

And it shall come about, if you listen obediently to my commandments which I am commanding you today, to love the Lord your God and to serve Him with all your heart and all your soul, that I will give the rain for your land in its season, the early and late rain, that you may gather in your grain and your new wine and your oil.

And I will give grass in your fields for your cattle, and you shall eat and be satisfied. Beware, lest your hearts be deceived and you turn away and serve other gods and worship them. Or the anger of the Lord will be kindled against you, and He will shut up the heavens so that there will be no rain and the ground will not yield its fruit; and you will perish quickly from the good land which the Lord is giving you. You shall

therefore impress these
words of mine on your
heart and on your soul; and
you shall bind them as a
sign on your hand, and they
shall be as frontals on your
forehead. And you shall
teach them to your sons,
talking of them when you
sit in your house and when
you walk along the road
and when you lie down and
when you rise up. And you
shall write them on the
doorposts of your house
and on your gates, so that
your days and the days of
your sons may be multi-
plied on the land which the
Lord swore to your fathers
to give them, as long as the
heavens remain above the
earth (Deuteronomy 11:
13-21).

As Jesus recited these texts, Joseph secured
the arm case, which was placed above the bend of
the left arm, where it would press against the
heart, giving effect to the Commandment, "And
these words, which I command thee this day, shall

be in thy heart." Then Joseph made a knot out of the thongs in the shape of the letter *Yodh;* the rest he wound around the boy's arm until it ended at his middle finger.

The case for the head was made of cowhide. It had four compartments containing separate pieces of parchment on which the same four texts were inscribed. On the outside of this case was the letter *Shin*. The case was sewn to a similar base and had the same thong as the other. It was placed on the boy's forehead and the strap was knotted in the shape of the letter *Daleth*. The ends hung forward over the shoulders. These three letters: *Shin*, *Daleth* and *Yodh*, made up the consonants of the Divine Name, *Shaddai*, the Almighty.

Mary was skilled in the art of dyeing. As wool came from the sheep, she washed it with wood ashes and then dyed it before spinning. For this purpose she used the murex shell from Tyre and indigo from India for the deep blue. For dyeing yellow she used almond leaves, and pomegranate bark supplied her with black, while green grapes pressed with water made a beautiful lush green. The new Talith was woven of the finest wool with beautiful multi-colored stripes.

As Jesus wore now for the first time the phylacteries with the *Tephillin*, the leather strips falling over the shoulders, wrapped into the big Talith, the old familiar prayers took on a new meaning, and a strange, deep emotion stirred his soul. After evening prayer Joseph turned to him and said, "Shalom, Jesus, son of David."

This was in the middle of the winter and Jesus would have to wait three months for the Feast of the Passover. How his heart longed for the House of God! The next time he came to Jerusalem he would be a "son of the Law," no longer subject to his parents.

This twelfth birthday terminated his school years. Now whenever he had some free time in the evenings, for instance, when the sun came out for a little while in these rainy months, he would climb up the hill behind the town. There he would stand and look toward the south, toward Jerusalem with the House of the Lord. And the great hunger of his soul to be again in his Father's House became almost unbearable.

9

THE SON OF THE LIVING GOD

To go from Nazareth to Jerusalem was to follow one of three routes. One might take the direct road due south across the rolling plain of Esdralon, then up into the hills of Samaria and over to the mountains of Judea. The distance being about 85 miles, a journey of four or five days on foot. This road was not always safe because the Samaritans were very bigoted and resented anyone's passing through their territory with faces set toward Jerusalem.

There was always a second caravan going around Passover time with all those who wanted to avoid Samaria altogether by traveling to the eastern bank of the Jordan, through the country of the Decapolis, and crossing into Judea near Jericho, but this way the length of the journey was almost doubled.

Then there was a third possibility: to go west to the seashore, pass by Mt. Carmel and follow the old caravan route which leads from Damascus into Egypt. Near Lydda one would have to leave the highway and go on footpaths through the Judean Mountains to Jerusalem.

When Jesus was a young boy his parents used to take the shortest road through Samaria. Later, after he went to school and could walk, when his father no longer bothered with the donkey they went alternately one year on the eastern banks of the Jordan and another year on the seashore so that they might view the beautiful country.

This year, when they asked Joseph whether he had any special choice, it is quite possible that he chose the shortest route, although he knew that traveling through Samaria might be quite disagreeable again. The little country between native Galilee and the mountainous Judea was inhabited by a strange people.

After the fall of the Northern Kingdom in 722 B.C., the Assyrians had taken most of the Jews away with them into captivity. In order to repopulate the country, they sent colonists over from Assur and settled them between Galilee and Judea. Gentiles by birth, they were soon no longer Gentiles in religion. They adopted the faith of the Israelites who had remained in the country, intermarrying with them. They took the Five Books of Moses for their scared scriptures. But there they stopped. They were not willing to accept either the authority of the Prophets or the traditions so dear to the Pharisees. In Jerusalem they were regarded as dangerous heretics. While they worshipped the same God as the Jews, read the same *Torah* and regarded Moses as their supreme law-giver, they were nevertheless more hated than the Gentiles. The Samaritans in turn hated the Jews. Finally they were solemnly excommunicated in the name of Jahweh.

They built a rival temple on Mount Gerizim and appointed their own high priest, who gathered around him priests and Levites. They married pagan women. The Jews broke off all relations, and the old traditional hatred was revived in all its bitterness. In Jesus' time the relations between his people and the Samaritans were worse than ever. To call a man "a Samaritan" was the gravest insult. A Jew would only say that when he had exhausted his vocabulary.

At the border before entering Samaria the leader of the pilgrimage would solemnly remind the pilgrims: "The Samaritan land is clean, the water is clean, the habitations are clean and the roads are clean," meaning that Samaria is a part of the Holy Land and it might be traversed without the risk of becoming liturgically unclean.

But this year nothing made any impression

on Jesus, neither the happy commotion of the start of the pilgrimage, nor any of the many little incidents along the road. His mind was filled with but one thought: the Temple. That was the place where his Heavenly Father dwelt. There alone one could offer sacrifice. The spotless lambs would be slaughtered again and burned at the entrance of the Holy House.

With every step closer to the Holy City he felt the attraction toward the House of God as he had never felt it before. Here we touch on the great mystery in the life of Jesus, unfathomable to any human mind, known in the church always as hypostatic union.

Since the first moment of his earthly existence he had known himself as saying "Father" not to Joseph but to one within him. Even while he was sitting at the feet of Joseph, or his teacher in the synagogue, learning to read and memorizing the Law and the Prophets he knew himself as being one with the Father.

While he was increasing "in wisdom, age and grace before God and man" he possessed all treasures of wisdom and knowledge through that unchanging union with the Father who is God.

As he now crossed through the huge Court of the Gentiles, he comprehended its deep significance: this Court was a sign that all nations from the earth had been called to adore the one true God, the creator of heaven and earth. Then he came to the low wall where tablets warned in Latin and Greek: No Gentile may enter under penalty of death. With holy awe he went through the barrier and hurried up the steps which brought him to the great altar of sacrifice. It was streaming with blood. On the day before the *Pasch* thousands of lambs were being slaughtered. There was blood and nothing but blood. He knew all these sacrifices were nothing but a symbol for the one sacrifice that was to come. As he looked up toward the entrance of the Holy House with its mysterious curtain behind which dwelt the Living God, there was only one wish in his heart: to remain there in the Temple forever, to be sacrificed and consumed instead of all those lambs; to give his last drop of blood that the Father might take away the sins of the world.

And the Father accepted now his offerings, but this time He commanded only one thing: that when the days of the feast should be over, when it was time to leave again for Nazareth he must stay behind and spend three days in the Temple.

He could not do otherwise than to fulfill the word which the Father had given him. The hours which he spent facing the House of Gold, completely lost in contemplation, flew like so many moments.

Then the Father sent him to the doctors. Within the great Temple enclosure, in one of the famous porticos, the learned doctors of the Law lectured all day during the days of the feast, and as long as crowds lingered behind. For those living far from Jerusalem this was the only opportunity to hear famous men explaining the Law.

It was quite customary for young people to ask questions of the experts of the Law, and these men loved to be consulted. But the questions the Father bade him ask were such that only He and the Son knew the answer. There were intricate points of the Law and complicated Paschal questions. Then the most pressing problem of all was discussed: the coming of the Messiah in the light of the Prophets.

At first the scribes were merely interested, but when none of the leading rabbis of Israel could find an answer, Jesus gave crystal-clear explanations, revealing a most profound understanding. They began to ask one another, "Who is this boy whose accent gives him away as a Galilean? Where did he acquire his profound knowledge. Never before did anyone speak like this boy!"

After the crowd was dismissed, they invited him into their company. They wanted to hear more of the things of God.

It was thus that, after three days, his parents found him in the Temple sitting in the midst of the doctors. Day and night Joseph had been cruelly tortured by the thought that not only had they lost him, but also that he had lost them and must have been trying to rejoin them. Now, finding him like this, they felt immediately that he was another Son in another world. Mary knew he had not lost them. He had left them deliberately. She said to him, "Son, why have you done so to us? Behold your father and I have sought you sorrowing."

Never in all those twelve years had he given them any reason for grief. It hurt him deeply when he had to answer in a way he knew would make them sad: "How is it that you sought me. Did you not know that I must be in my Father's House, about my Father's business?"

Poor Joseph! He who in all these years had been called "father," had now to hear his son in front of everybody refer to God as his true Father. Jesus put all the love and gratitude and admiration he had for Mary and Joseph into the tone of his voice, and into the look of his eyes, to console them in this moment.

Then his time was over. He rose, shalomed reverently before the venerable elders, as became one of his age, and went with his parents to Nazareth.

How quickly the gossip had traveled ahead and met them as they returned home. Inquisitive neighbors and cousins rushed to their door to besiege the poor parents with questions: "Where did you find him? What did he do? How long did you search for him? Is it true that he was sitting with the doctors? What did he mean when he said he must be about his Father's business?''

Mary and Joseph could not deny any of it. And so it happened that the young man's stay in the Temple was not only a manifestation of himself to the doctors, but also a revelation to his mother and Joseph, and to all his relatives. Not all of them would take it in good faith.

It touched him to the heart to see with what great humility Mary and Joseph waited for what he was going to do. Perhaps he must be about his Father's business from now on and take up the career of a rabbi . . . ? They watched anxiously to see whether he would now put his things in order and take leave to spend his days with the scribes in the Temple, according to the old saying, "Anyone who wants to assume riches should go to Galilee, but he who wants to strive for wisdom has to go to Judea.''

When he simply resumed his daily duties as if nothing had happened, helping his mother in the morning with the water and with the turning of the grindstone and, later on, spent his hours with Joseph in the workshop, their apprehension left them slowly.

How he admired Mary and Joseph in their complete submission to the will of God! The shock and the pain of the three days loss, the terrible searching, they remembered it all, not with resentment, but with joy. What a privilege to have been allowed a glimpse into the secret of the Divine Son and his Heavenly Father and to accept the suffering that such knowledge involved. The Father had taught them the great lesson: "He who loves father and mother more than me is not worthy of me."

10

WHEN THE KING WAS CARPENTER

And now it was the will of the Heavenly Father that Jesus should devote most of his time to learning Joseph's trade, that he should become a carpenter and a carpenter's son. "Love labor and teach it to your sons," the Rabbi Shenaiah had said.

As a small boy Jesus had learned by watching; now he began to share the important decisions of a mature craftsman. Father and son went together to select lumber, large logs brought in by woodcutters from the wooded hills around Nazareth. The choice was always difficult, and from Joseph, Jesus learned to appreciate the beauty of sycamores and poplars, terebinth, olive, chestnut, or oak. He must pick logs which would be good for doors or window-frames; he must select slender rods to be made into handles. He learned too, that some of the worst of crimes were to cut down a tree which belonged to someone else, and to call a man a *Qoses ben Quses*, a "cutter and a son of a cutter," was almost as bad as calling him a "Samaritan," and one must never buy from such a person.

Back at home, Joseph showed Jesus how to fasten the new log to the carpenter's bench, how to hew it roughly into shape with hatchet, broad axe, and saw, or how to work it with a plane. Sometimes their tools were hammers, mallet, and chisel. Sometimes the vise, the plummet, and its cord were more important.

In this way Jesus learned also cabinet-making, as the father carpenter showed him how to create household furniture such as cedar chests, cupboards, window frames, door frames, or low tables and all kinds of farm implements.

Nazareth was a small country town surrounded by little farms, so there were frequent calls to repair tools around the neighboring slopes and hills. Together father and son produced handles for pitch forks, threshing blades, hoes, wooden yokes for oxen, and wooden plows, and also learned to help in the construction of house frames, handling the large heavy beams, or making roofs with a layer of thorns and clay.

Much skill and strong labor were needed to work such rough timber into beams or plows.

As the two carpenters worked side by side in the courtyard, their heads covered against the burning sun, the young man Jesus may have said lovingly to Joseph, "My Father in Heaven, the builder of the universe, has given me on earth a father who is a builder also." Joseph, stopping to lean on a half-worked plow, may perhaps have answered, "The first king in Israel was taken from behind the plow; another was called from the sheepfold; and the second David, the Messiah of Israel, will come from a carpenter's shop."

11

"OUT OF THE ABUNDANCE OF THE HEART"

A group much berated in local talk were the priests at Jerusalem. What embittered the people most was that these authorities in Jerusalem did not conceal their contempt for Galileans. Loftily they announded that no Galilean was well versed in the Law, and that their Aramaic dialect was nothing short of ridiculous. Galileans were simply comical "northerners."

About this, the "northerners" found much to say among themselves. As long as Jesus was a small child, his parents sent him away whenever such talk occurred or criticism of the chief priests began. Mary and Joseph felt very keenly that even if priests did not live up to their high office they were nevertheless the first servants of the Most High. After Jesus' twelfth birthday, however, he was allowed to stay. In silence he listened to remarks on the accumulation of wealth through shady transactions in the Temple, on the lack of faith of so many who were Sadducees and did not believe in life after death, and especially on their treacherous compromising with the Roman authorities. Many an elaborate tale was recounted with relish: the chief priests were taking what should have gone to another of lower rank; they were visiting the threshing floors to get a much larger amount of the harvest than what was due them; they had been beating the people with rods within the very Temple grounds.

In the hot summer months most families would ascend to their flat rooftops to catch the cool evening breeze, and very animated conversations would go on from roof to roof. There was one topic in which all children were most interested: news of any recent caravan which had passed outside of Nazareth. From the hill behind the town, they could often see after the rainy season, great caravans coming and going on the old route from Babylon into Egypt.

In Seluceia on the Tigris River there was a large Jewish population which had a flourishing trade with Alexandria, in Egypt. Caravans of fifty camels and more, passed by Nazareth from Damascus to Alexandria. The return trip always followed the coastal road for about 30 days, all the way to Antioch. From there they would cross the desert, taking about twice the time again to reach home.

These large caravans traveled on dirt roads baked by the sun and hardened by traffic. The bridges over streams and rivers were kept in repair by the Roman government and there were always hundreds of Roman soldiers along the way, the best protection against robbers.

Whenever such a large caravan was in sight, men from Nazareth would go to meet and trade with the camel drivers. In the evening, from rooftop to rooftop, they told of what they had heard and seen: of furs and hides from Persia, of embroideries and carpets, beautifully-carved ivory work and pottery. There would be silks in all colors from China, and perfumes, rugs and pearls from India. Sometimes there were even tigers from India, which, together with lions from the jungle on the Jordan, would be sent to Rome for the games in the Coliseum.

On the return trip from Alexandria there would be papyrus, parchments, and beautifully-copied scrolls of the Scriptures. Rich men in both Egypt and Babylon arranged regular caravans for which one could buy a ticket, and travelers, students, or men with business in foreign parts often took the opportunity.

The broker who handled the arrangements did not travel with them. He was usually a wealthy man in Alexandria or Antioch, who managed several caravans. With the profits he would buy great vineyards and thousands of slaves, or hundreds of horses and camels which could then be rented to the travelers. Both the animals and the cargo of such a caravan were insured against loss, and these rich brokers had their own inns at certain intervals, always near a fort or a town where the caravans might pitch tent, or pitch camp at night.

Small children in Nazareth were curious and intrigued to learn that one merchant in the caravan had sets of false teeth to be sold in the bazaars in Jerusalem. At the next feast in the Holy City they searched eagerly around the marketplace until they found what they sought: animal or human teeth fastened together with gold bands and filled with cement!

But even talk about a caravan, however it might excite childish imaginations, would often end in petty complaints from those who envied the rich, and cursed their own fate which had put them into modest circumstances.

James and Jude, the two favorite cousins of Jesus of Nazareth, were often with him, as together they silently listened to such argument and discussion among the elders. Afterwards they would come to talk among themselves of how very difficult it is not to sin with the tongue. James frequently quoted a favorite proverb:

"Death and life are in the power of the tongue and everyone shall eat the fruit thereof."

And a fitting end to such discussion would be: "If any man offend not in word, the same is a perfect man," or, "Let us storm heaven for the perfect man to come—our Messiah-King." For all conversations and all discussions would always point to the one most important subject—the coming of the Messiah.

12

THE SHADOW OF THE CROSS

The Messiah was the hope of an invaded country longing for the end of Roman rule and Roman culture. One generation before Jesus was born Roman legions had marched across Syria, taking the little kingdom of Judea by force and incorporating it into the mighty Roman Empire, which at that time comprised almost the whole of the then-known world. The many diverse races retained much of their own culture, customs and religion, but Roman law, Roman governors and Roman legions united them all.

As with other invaded countries, so it happened to little Palestine: first came the soldiers of the occupation army, then soon afterward their families with teachers who brought another culture and another religion into the country known as the "Holy Land of the Chosen People."

The Romans had only Greek teachers, usually slaves, for their children. The Greek language was predominantly spoken and a Greco-Roman civilization spread rapidly over the little land. Pagan games and sports were introduced to the young people; pagan ideas and ideals were taught. The many Gentiles who lived in Galilee were easily won to such innovations and, worst of all, Herod the King could not be outdone in servility. He wanted to have a good name with the Romans. He therefore built a marble temple to the Roman god, Panias. He called his new capital "Caesarea." He rebuilt the city of Samaria, and gave it the name Sebaste, the Greek word for Augustus. He favored the new religion and the new philosophy wherever he could.

In Palestine, teachers and rabbis were greatly worried. They tried to keep children away from the sports and games, and occupy them with an even more strict religious training and religious services. But in spite of all their vigilance, the pagan influence told more and more upon their young people.

The elders of the nation found their sole consolation therefore in the thought of the coming of the Messiah. All gloom would disappear from their faces as they talked in eager anticipation of the revolution the Messiah would bring about. More than any other generation, Jesus and his schoolmates were trained to find all references to the Messiah-King in the books of the Law and the Prophets.

The teaching about the Messiah is fundamental in the Old Testament. In the first book of Genesis God said to the serpent, "And I will put enmity between you and the woman, and between your seed and her seed; he shall bruise you on the head, and you shall bruise him on the heel" (3:15).

In the same book are the special prophecies that through the descendants of Abraham, Isaac and Jacob all people of the earth shall be blessed.

Yet occasionally the young students wondered, *Was not the Messiah to suffer for His people? What of the prophecies of Isaiah and Jeremiah?* Their teacher's firm assurance that the Messiah would be above all the King of kings, that He might have nothing personally to do with misery and suffering, did not entirely convince them all. More than one reread for himself the prophecies of the Holy Scripture.

Children memorized the prophecy of Balaam, "A star shall come forth from Jacob, and a scepter shall rise from Israel, and shall crush through the forehead of Moab, and tear down all the sons of Sheth . . . . One from Jacob shall have dominion" (Numbers 24:17-19).

The fifth book of Moses describes the Messiah as a prophet like unto himself (Moses):

"And the Lord said to me, they have spoken well. I will raise up a prophet from among their country-men like you, and I will put My words in his mouth, and he shall speak to them all that I command Him" (Deuteronomy 18:18).

If the Messianic prophecies in these early books were still somewhat general, they became much more individual and more specific in the time of the kings, when the Messiah is described as the "Son of David, King and Victor" and, he is shown obviously to be a person. Teachers had their classes recite Psalm Two which describes how the Messiah, although surrounded by enemies, conquers them all:

> "Why are the nations in
> an uproar, and the peoples
> devising a vain thing? The
> kings of the earth take
> their stand, and the rulers
> take counsel together a-
> gainst the Lord and against
> His Anointed: Let us tear
> their fetters apart, and cast
> away their cords from us!
> He who sits in the heavens
> laughs, the Lord scoffs at
> them. Then He will speak
> to them in His anger and
> terrify them in His fury:

120

But as for Me, I have in-
stalled My King upon Zion,
My holy mountain. I will
surely tell of the decree of
the Lord: He said to Me,
Thou art My Son, today I
have begotten Thee. Ask
of Me, and I will surely give
the nations as Thine in-
heritance, and the very
ends of the earth as Thy
possession. Thou shalt
break them with a rod of
iron, Thou shalt shatter
them like earthenware"
(2:1-9).

The young students had to learn Psalm 72:

Give the king Thy judg-
ments, O God, and Thy
righteousness to the king's
son. May he judge Thy
people with righteousness,
and Thine afflicted with
justice. Let the mountains
bring peace to the people,
and the hills in righteousness. May he vindicate the
afflicted of the people, save

the children of the needy, and crush the oppressor.

Let them fear Thee while the sun endures, and as long as the moon, throughout all generations. May he come down like rain upon the mown grass, like showers that water the earth. In his days may the righteous flourish, and abundance of peace till the moon is no more.

May he also rule from sea to sea, and from the river to the ends of the earth. Let the nomads of the desert bow before him; and his enemies lick the dust. Let the kings of Tarshish and the islands bring presents; the kings of Sheba and Seba offer gifts. And let all kings bow down before him, all nations serve him.

For he will deliver the needy when he cries for help, the afflicted also, and him who has no helper. He will have compassion on the poor and needy, and the lives of the needy he will save. He will rescue their life from oppression and violence; and their blood will be precious in his sight; so may he live; and may the gold of Sheba be given to him; and let them pray for him continually; let them bless him all day long.

May there be abundance of grain in the earth on top of the mountains; its fruit will wave like the cedars of Lebanon; and may those from the city flourish like vegetation of the earth. May his name endure forever; may his name increase as long as the sun shines; and let men bless themselves by him; let all nations call him blessed (1-17).

With great pride the teacher explained that the Messiah would be not only a prophet and a king, but a priest forever; and the children were required to learn Psalm 110:1-7:

> "The Lord says to my Lord: 'Sit at My right hand, until I make Thine enemies a footstool for Thy feet.' The Lord will stretch forth Thy strong scepter from Zion, saying, 'Rule in the midst of Thine enemies.' Thy people will volunteer freely in the day of Thy power; in holy array, from the womb of the dawn, Thy youth are to Thee as the dew.
>
> "The Lord has sworn and will not change His mind, 'Thou art a priest forever according to the order of Melchizedek.' The Lord is at Thy right hand; he will shatter kings in the day of His wrath. He will judge among the nations, he will fill them with corpses, he will shatter the chief men over a broad country. He will drink from

the brook by the wayside;
therefore He will lift up
His head."

They learned where the Messiah would be born because thus it is written in the Prophet Micah 5:2: "But as for you, Bethlehem Ephrathah, too little to be among the clans of Judah, from you One will go forth for Me to be ruler in Israel. His goings forth are from long ago, from the days of eternity."

They heard that He would come through a mother, not through a human father. The Prophet Isaiah said: "Behold, a young woman shall be with child and bear a son, and she shall call his name Immanuel" (7:14).

The great Prophet Jeremiah said about the Messiah: "Behold, the days are coming, declares the Lord, when I shall raise up for David a righteous Branch; and He will reign as king and act wisely and do justice and righteousness in the land" (23:5).

A little later Isaiah prophesies of Cyrus as a figure of the Christ, the great deliverer of God's people: "Thus says the Lord to Cyrus His anointed, whom I have taken by the right hand, to subdue nations before him, and to loose the loins of kings; to open doors before him so that gates will not be shut: I will go before you and make the rough places smooth; I will shatter the doors of bronze and cut through these iron bars. And I will give you the treasures of darkness, and hidden wealth of secret places, in order that you may know that it is I, the Lord, the God of Israel, who calls you by your name . . . . Drip down, O heavens from above, and let the clouds pour down righteousness; let the earth open up and salvation bear fruit, and righteousness spring up with it. I the Lord have created it" (45:1-3, 8).

The Prophet Ezekiel adds a new consoling feature in describing the Messiah as a good shepherd: "Then I will set over them one shepherd, my servant David, and he will feed them; he will feed them himself and be their shepherd. And I, the Lord, will be their God . . ." (34:23-24a).

Even the younger boys noticed that the passages their teacher chose to be memorized had always to do with the Messiah as a King in triumph and victory, and splendor and glory, as in Daniel 2:44: ". . . the God of heaven will set up a kingdom which will never be destroyed, and that kingdom will not be left for another people; it will crush and put an end to all these kingdoms, but it will itself endure forever."

Or from the Prophet Haggai: "The latter glory of this house will be greater than the former, says the Lord of hosts, and in this place I shall give peace, declares the Lord of hosts" (2:9).

After his twelfth birthday, when Jesus was declared "Son before the Law," he had stopped going to elementary school, and now the higher studies began. On Mondays, Thursdays and on the Sabbath the young men would sit at the feet of the teacher, being instructed in the writings of the great rabbis.

The years passed. At eighteen Jesus entered the marriageable age and on his twentieth birthday he reached maturity before the State.

What he had learned about the Messiah, either in school or by listening to the older men, could be summed up as: The Messiah-King would set up a world government with Judaism as the universal religion; he would punish the enemies in Gehenna but he would lead the land to great national prosperity; all the exiled Jews would be called home and there would be a great reunion; from then on there would be peace between men and beasts, and peace between men and men.

This materialistic kingdom of great prosperity and glory—which would be such a contrast to present slavery and oppression—that was all the people expected of the Messiah to come. Impatiently they waited for the return of Elias which would be the sign of the approach of the great change: the sun would break up, the moon would turn into blood, in the sky swords would appear and the great voice of God would shake· the foundations of the earth.

Through the hard labor of years, the family of Joseph had saved enough to buy all the "Sacred

Books," scroll by scroll, and in the evenings or on the Sabbath afternoons, they would take turns reading aloud to each other.

Then, Mary and her son saw Joseph begin to fail. Suddenly and quite rapidly, his physical strength ebbed, while during the Scripture readings, his features would take on a hue and a glow as though a fire were burning within him. Solemnly, the lines of the scrolls foretold that the Messiah, besides being a priest forever, would also be a man of sorrow. In Isaiah they read, "He has no stately form or majesty that we should look upon Him, nor appearance that we should be attracted to Him. He was despised and forsaken of men, a man of sorrows, and acquainted with grief; and like one from whom men hide their face, He was despised, and we did not esteem Him" (53:2a-3).

They turned again to the words of the Psalmist:

> My God, my God, why hast Thou forsaken me? Far from my deliverance are the words of my groaning. O my God, I cry by day, but Thou dost not answer; and by night, but I find no rest. Yet Thou art holy, O Thou who art enthroned upon the praises

of Israel. In Thee our fathers trusted; they trusted, and Thou didst deliver them. To Thee they cried out, and were delivered; in Thee they trusted, and were not disappointed.

But I am a worm, and not a man, a reproach of men, and despised by the people. All who see me sneer at me; they separate with the lip, they wag the head, saying, "Commit yourself to the Lord; let Him deliver him; let Him rescue him, because He delights in him.

Yet Thou art He who didst bring me forth from the womb, thou didst make me trust when upon my mother's breasts. Upon Thee I was cast from birth; Thou hast been my God from my mother's womb.

Be not far from me, for trouble is near; for there is none to help. Many bulls have surrounded me;

strong bulls of Bashan have
encircled me. They open
wide their mouth at me, as
ravening and a roaring lion.
I am poured out like water,
and all my bones are out
of joint; my heart is like
wax; it is melted within
me. My strength is dried
up like a potsherd, and my
tongue cleaves to my jaws;
and Thou dost lay me in
the dust of death. For dogs
have surrounded me; a
band of evildoers have en-
compassed me; they
pierced my hands and my
feet. I can count all my
bones. They look, they
stare at me; they divide my
garments among them, and
for my clothing they cast
lots (22:1-18).

The sacred writings had revealed the true
story of the Anointed One of God, the King of
kings, the Prince of Peace: yes, He would be a
King, but his crown would not be one of gold,
but one of suffering; yes, He would reign from a
throne—not bedecked with jewels, but made of

wood shaped in the form of a cross; yes, He would conquer the universe, but only after He had gone through the dark gate of death because His Kingdom would not be of this world.

After such moments in their little home there was always a great silence. A flame *was* burning within Joseph, and his weakness became more apparent. With each new reading, the fire of love and compassion was kindled, consuming him as the holocaust on the great altar in the Temple was consumed by sacrificial fire. No word was said, no question was asked, it was not necessary. But in the shadow of the wood-shaped cross, three hearts were burning with love—love for one another, love for the Eternal Father in Heaven who had ordained it all, Whose name be praised, Whose Holy name will be adored.

13

THE HIDDEN LIFE

When Joseph died, Mary and Jesus wept.
She had lost her husband, her guardian, her best
friend who had loved her with such an utterly
unselfish love.

Jesus had grown to admire and love this
"just man" who had always been so faithful
and unselfish, so devoted and loyal, so obedient
to the will of the Father, and so loving to his
family and friends. No one ever would be nearer
and dearer. Now he was gone. His spirit "was
carried by the angels into Abraham's bosom."
There Joseph, the silent, the just, the humble,
would meet the company of the just who had
preceded him. There he would be greeted by the
spirits of Adam and Eve, of Abraham, Isaac and
Jacob, of King David his glorious ancestor, and

by the spirits of the little children who had died because the cruel Herod had wanted to kill the Messiah. There too were the spirits of Zacharias and Elisabeth, of Joachim his father-in-law and Anna his mother. Together they rejoiced that "the salvation was at hand" and peacefully they waited their ascension into heaven.

After the burial, Mary and Jesus returned home and began their new life together. The young man took over his heritage: the house and the courtyard (this was considered a separate piece of property), and all the household utensils belonged now to him. At the same time he assumed all the responsibilities as the head of a family and his mother's protector. As her grown-up son, he had to support and represent his mother. With Joseph's death he had become "the master of the house." Mary's duties continued to be the same: grinding meal and baking bread, carrying water and gathering fuel, spinning and weaving, cooking and washing.

Jesus replaced Joseph in the workshop and became the carpenter of Nazareth in the everyday routine of living—*ora et labora*—prayer and work.

"Verily Thou art a hidden God, O Saviour," the Prophet Isaiah had cried. The poor home in an obscure country town, the ordinary occupation as an artisan and the simple family life were chosen by the Heavenly Father that the Son might teach his brethren the one important lesson: perfection consists in doing ordinary things extraordinarily well.

God wanted the Son's life on earth to be not that of a hermit on a rugged mountain, but life in a family circle in a little house, between many houses, on a street in a small town. A social life in daily contacts with human beings, daily business, daily greetings, daily dealings with customers.

The great glory of these long silent years of the hidden life was the togetherness between mother and son. To understand this one must go back to the very earliest days of creation when God had created man according to His own image and likeness as man and woman. When Adam and Eve, clothed with the light as with a mantle, lived before God as holy children with their father.

Jesus and his mother lived together in the same house, but no words were needed, their souls were always closely united. And so together they advanced in wisdom and grace before God and man.

During all those years the mother saw her son, who was also the Son of God, working busily in a carpenter shop. She watched him saw and plane, receive orders and deliver the finished work, year after year. How much longer would that continue? In what way would the redemption of mankind from their sins be finally accomplished? How would the Messiah manifest himself to his people? And where was John, the son of her cousin Elisabeth? According to the word, of his father Zacharias he was to be precursor. He was to prepare the people for the coming of the Messiah. And when would all that come to pass that old Simeon had prophesied to her?

There was no answer to her silent questions, but that did not disturb her. She contemplated all these things in her heart and she persevered in silence as the handmaid of the Lord.

It would have only been natural that out of a genuine anxiety she might have spoken, but she had learned not to ask questions. Now she knew that her Son had to be about His Father's business and this knowledge was sufficient. When the Father wished it, He would make it clear that his hour had come. Until then she remained in peace and quiet repose.

"You shall bring forth a son," the Archangel Gabriel had said to her, "and you shall name him Jesus. He will be great, and will be called the Son of the Most High; and the Lord God will give Him the throne of His father David; and He will reign over the house of Jacob forever . . ." (Lk. 1:31b, 33a). And here was her son making ploughshares and other farm tools.

"And you, child, will be called the prophet of the Most High," old Zacharias had addressed

136

his new-born son, "for you will go on BEFORE THE LORD TO PREPARE HIS WAYS; to give to His people the knowledge of salvation by the forgiveness of their sins" (Luke 1:76-77).

For a long time no one had had word from John who had vanished in the desert. ". . . Behold, this Child is appointed for the fall and rise of many in Israel, and for a sign to be opposed . . ." (Luke 2:34).

Simeon had addressed Mary in the Temple: "yea a sword will pierce even your own soul—to the end that thoughts from many hearts may be revealed." As Mary pondered on the fate of the Messiah, as she learned it from Holy Scriptures, this mysterious sword pierced her heart ever deeper and deeper.

The hidden life of Jesus at Nazareth was full of hidden suffering, but it was also filled with that one great hidden joy: to do the will of the Father! For this Jesus came into the world, and this is what he had to preach, first, through thirty years of silent example.

Between his twentieth and thirtieth years he went to Jerusalem for all the big feasts. Each time he became more keenly aware that the house of His Father, the holy Temple, was being desecrated and made into a den of thieves. When he listened to the teachings of the rabbis in the Hall of Solomon, or in the cloisters of the Royal Porch, he perceived each time more keenly how shallow and hair-splitting their doctrine had become, how they misunderstood the great commandment of the Sabbath, how ridiculous were their thousands of petty rules, how completely they had forgotten that the Sabbath was for men, and not men for the Sabbath. He knew that one day he must act. He was ready, waiting for the Father to give the sign, but the Father remained silent. His hour had not yet come. In these years he learned how hard it is for the human heart to wait. "Not my will, but Thy will be done" became his constant prayer. And no one knew the hour but the Father.

14

THE HOUR

Then the news was brought to Nazareth that a great prophet was preaching in the wilderness of the Jordan, and his name was John. "Do repentance, because the Kingdom of God is at hand" was his message.

Mary understood and renewed her surrender to the holy will of the Father. The word on the lips of the Son of man were, "You have called me—behold here I am!"

Mary must have expected it when Jesus asked her whether he might accompany her to her sister's house.

He shouldered the chest with her belongings and they left the house where they had spent so many peaceful years. His mother did not even linger to throw a glance over the courtyard and house. She had "laid her hand on the plow and did not look back."

Jesus entrusted her into the care of her sister's family and then bade them farewell. No one asked him where he was going.

The Spirit of the Heavenly Father led him to join John the Prophet and ask for his baptism. "Then Jesus arrived from Galilee at the Jordan coming to John, to be baptized by him. But John tried to prevent Him, saying, 'I have need to be baptized by You, and You come to me?' But Jesus answering said to him, 'Permit it at this time; for in this way it is fitting for us to fulfill all righteousness'" (Matthew 3:13-15). And, as he stepped out of the waters of the river, the voice of the Father, hitherto known only to the Son, made itself heard to all generations of man: THOU ART MY BELOVED SON. IN THEE I AM WELL PLEASED.

The Spirit of God descending upon him in the shape of a dove, led him from his hidden life into the desert of temptation, and from there into the world of men. He was to bring the words of the Father to men that they might come to believe and to know that He and the Father are one and that we who see Him also see the Father.

BIBLIOGRAPHY

A Treasury of Jewish Holidays, Hyman E. Goldin

Biblischer Altagzeit Des Alten Testaments, E. W. Heaton, Claudius Verlag, Munchen

Daily Life In The Times of Jesus, Henri Daniel-Rops, Mentor-Omega Book, The New American Library, New York, NY 10019

Der Menschensohn, Peter Lippert, S.J.

Das Leben Jesus Im Lande Und Volke Israel, Dr. Franz Michel William, Heber & Co., G.M.B.H. Derlagsbuch-handlung

Encyclopedia of Bible Life, Madeleine E. Miller and J. Lane Miller, Harper Brothers, New York, NY 10022

Jesus and His Times, Daniel-Rops, E.P., Dutton & Co., Inc., New York, NY 10003

Life of Christ, Mauriac

Life of Christ, Moritz, Meschler, S.J.

Life of Christ, Fr. Prat, S.J.

Life of Christ, Riccioti

Mary and Joseph, Denis O'Shea, The Bruce Publishing Co., New York, NY 10022

Pattern Divine, Fr. Temple, S.T.D., B. Herder Book Co.

The Ancient Way, Life and Landmarks of the Holy Land, Fr. J. Franklin Ewing, S.J., Charles Scribner's Sons, New York, NY 10017

The Holy Family, Denis O'Shea, C.C., M. H. Gill & Sons, Ltd.

The Lord, Romano Guardini, Henry Regnery Company, Chicago, Ill. 60601

To Know Christ, Frank J. Sheed, Christian Classics, Inc., Westminster, Md. 21157